Viewpoints: Japan and England

すっきり日英比較

Terry O'Brien
Kei Mihara
Shuyo Tatemoto
Hiroshi Kimura

NUN'UN-DO

Viewpoints: Japan and England

Terry O'Brien
Kei Mihara
Shuyo Tatemoto
Hiroshi Kimura

Download Audio

音声ファイル
無料 DL
のご案内

このテキストの音声を無料で視聴（ストリーミング）・ダウンロードできます。自習用音声としてご活用ください。
以下のサイトにアクセスしてテキスト番号で検索してください。

https://nanun-do.com　テキスト番号［**511633**］

※ 無線 LAN（WiFi）に接続してのご利用を推奨いたします。

※ 音声ダウンロードは Zip ファイルでの提供になります。
お使いの機器によっては別途ソフトウェア（アプリケーション）の導入が必要となります。

Read by

Michael Rhys
Bonnie Waycott

※ Viewpoints : Japan and England の音声ダウンロードページは
以下の QR コードからもご利用になれます。

はしがき

楽しく学ばねば英語は身に付きません。楽しく、わかりやすく、ためになると実感できる授業に接すれば英語力は次第に身に付いてきます。Viewpoints: Japan and England は、そのような趣旨に基づいて作成した総合教材で、初中級レベルの学習者を対象としたものです。

大学で英語を学ぶことは、ことばを媒介としたトレーニングだけではありません。それと併せて他の国と接触して自分の目を養うことが必要です。自国の常識が他国の非常識になる場合もあるからです。異文化に触れることで視野が広がり、新たな発見が生まれます。とりわけ感情を含めた他の国の人々の心を理解して、本当の意味での英語力が身に付いたと言えます。

本書は、季節、運転免許証、医療制度、休日、花火など幅広い日常的なテーマで、オブライエン氏が書き下ろした日英比較のエッセイを中心にしています。常識に疑問を投げかけ、日本とイギリス事情の様相を鋭い感性と客観的視点に基づいて比較し、しかも知的ユーモアを交えて明快に述べています。

まずは、軽妙な文体による 350 語程度で書かれたエッセイを楽しんでください。そして、TOEIC® テスト形式の文法や長文空所補充問題、リスニング問題などを通して、英語力をブラッシュアップしてくれることを願っています。

2015 年春　著者

本書の使い方

全体で 15 Lessons です。各 Lesson は本文（Reading）と、その内容理解度をチェックするための練習問題 (A)(B) があります。また本文と関連のある会話文や文法問題で構成しています。

Photographs

写真の説明となるように、与えられた文字で始まる単語を、空所

1 Reading

本文の内容理解と共に、CD を聞いてリスニング力を向上させてください。

A Vocabulary

定義に合う語を本文より探して書いてください。

B Comprehension

(1) 本文の内容理解度をチェックするために次の 3 つの形式のいずれかになっています。
- 空所に入る適切な語を語群より選んでください。　Lessons 1, 4, 7, 10, 13
- 前の英文に続く適切なものを選んでください。　Lessons 2, 5, 8, 11, 14
- 空所内の語句を正しく並べ替えてください。　Lessons 3, 6, 9, 12, 15

(2) 次に完成した英文の内容が述べられている段落の番号を［　］に書いてください。

2 Conversation

(A) CD を聞いて空所に単語を書き、会話を完成してください。
(B) CD を聞いて質問文を完成し、それに対する正しい答えを (A) ～ (D) から 1 つ選んでください。

3 Incomplete Sentences

短文を完成するため、空所に入る最も適切な語句を (A) ～ (D) から 1 つ選んでください。

4 Text Completion

長文を完成するため、空所に入る最も適切な語句を (A) ～ (D) から 1 つ選んでください。

5 Keywords

各 Lesson に出てきた語句の意味を確認してください。

Contents

Lesson 1 Heights

tenses (present tense, past tense, future tense)

Photographs

Describe the picture by filling in the blanks in these sentences.

1. Three police officers are (t   ) with each other while standing.
2. One of the police officers is standing apart (f   ) the others.

1 Reading

02

[1] I was pleased when I first arrived in Japan and found that I had grown during the journey here by about 20 centimetres. What I mean is that in England I was only just above the average height. That made me tall enough to become a policeman, so if I couldn't find any other employment, I always had something to fall back on.

[2] Now that I was living in Japan, I was taking the crowded trains in the mornings, but unlike most of my foreigner friends, I enjoyed it. In Japan, I was suddenly a lot taller than most other people. That's right ... I was looking down on everyone. From my viewpoint, the train car was a long sea of black hair.

[3] My new status of being taller than most people did come at a price, however. Doors were usually too low for me, and I lost count of how many times I came into painful contact with them. Shopping for clothes also proved to be a problem. The shirts pinched my armpits, and I gave up trying to fasten the cuff buttons. In winter I always had cold feet at night since the bedding was designed for the average Japanese person. Not surprisingly, I was beginning to regret my height.

[4] The rest of the story is probably not news to you. Today, the young generation has shot up alarmingly, so that now I am actually below average. Today's youth would never have fitted into yesterday's compact automobiles. There was no headroom and no leg room, so that putting on the brake required difficult contortions from the driver, which is not good if you need to stop in a hurry.

[5] In the 1970s, when many Japanese people were buying their first family car, there was nowhere to drive. One answer was to go up, and that's why there are so many mountain roads. But the thing is, there's little to see at the top except for a car park and maybe, an abandoned restaurant. People today are still going upwards, however. There is a rush to build skyscrapers, and, unlike in England, Japanese people love to live in high-rise apartments. Do you think that is a wise thing to do in an earthquake-prone country?

Notes fall back on「～に頼る」 come at a price「かなりの代償を払うことになる」 cuff button「カフスボタン」 shoot up「背が高くなる」 high-rise「高層の」 earthquake-prone「地震がよく起こる」

A Vocabulary

Find the words in the reading that match these definitions. Write the verbs and nouns in their base forms.

1. ________________ a way of thinking about or looking at a situation (line 7)
2. ________________ to press someone's skin tightly (line 11)
3. ________________ small and taking up very little space (line 17)
4. ________________ no longer being used or looked after (line 23)
5. ________________ a very tall modern city building (line 24)

B Comprehension

Complete each sentence with a word from the box. Then write the number of the paragraph where the information is found.

driving good high much policeman

1. Being tall was not always a ( ) thing because doors, clothes, and bedding didn't fit me. par. [ ]
2. In England I was tall enough to be a ( ), but in Japan I was suddenly way above average height. par. [ ]
3. People used to enjoy driving up mountain roads, but now they like to live in ( ) buildings. par. [ ]
4. Surprisingly, I liked taking the train in the mornings because I was ( ) taller than other people. par. [ ]
5. Young people today have become taller and would have had trouble ( ) old compact cars. par. [ ]

2 Conversation

(A) As you listen to the conversation, fill in the blanks. 03

Anne: Where do you live?

Brian: Right in the 1( ) of the city. We are on the 2( ) floor of a block of flats.

Anne: Do you like 3( ) so high up?

Brian: The building's 4( ) for shopping and transport, but I do miss having a garden.

Anne: Well, I couldn't live there at all because I'm 5( ) of heights.

(B) Listen and fill in the blanks in each question. Then choose the best answer. 04

1. Why does the man ______________ ____________ ______________?
   (A) It has a good view. (B) It is cheap.
   (C) It's convenient. (D) It's new.

2. Why doesn't the woman ______________ _________ ______________ in such a place?
   (A) It's in the city. (B) She can't stand high places.
   (C) It doesn't have a garden. (D) There's no lift.

Grammar Points: 時制

1. 現在時制：現在の動作・状態・習慣・事実

   I am a university student and study applied chemistry.（私は大学生で、応用化学を勉強しています）

   I usually get up at seven.（たいてい 7 時に起きます）

   London is the capital of the United Kingdom.（ロンドンはイギリスの首都です）

2. 過去時制：過去の動作・状態・習慣・事実

   I lived in Manchester three years ago.（3 年前はマンチェスターに住んでいました）

   I often played tennis when I was in my early teens.（10 代前半のとき、よくテニスをしました）

   Isaac Newton formulated the law of universal gravitation.
   （アイザック・ニュートンは万有引力の法則を定式化しました）

3. 未来時制：未来の予定・予想、話し手の意志

   I will visit my grandparents this weekend.（今週末、祖父母のところに行く予定です）

   It is going to rain this afternoon.（今日の午後、雨が降るでしょう）

   I will never give up.（絶対あきらめません）

3 Incomplete Sentences

Choose the correct word or phrase to complete each sentence.

1. I usually ________ to school but yesterday I took a train.
   (A) have walked (B) walk (C) walked (D) will walk

2. I expect my brother ________ taller than me in a year or so.
   (A) has been (B) is (C) was (D) will be

3. My sister ________ part-time, but now she has a full-time job.
   (A) is working (B) will be work (C) worked (D) works

4. I don't want to live in a high-rise apartment as I ________ afraid of heights.
   (A) am (B) don't (C) was (D) will be

5. I ________ food in stock in case a big earthquake hits the city I live in.
   (A) had (B) have been (C) have (D) will be

4 Text Completion

Select the best answers to complete the text.

At the weekend my mountain-climbing friends and I went to the Northern Alps. The six of us ________ to hike from the ropeway station and along the ridge to a

1. (A) want
   (B) wants
   (C) wanted
   (D) won't

mountain-top lodge. We ________ something like this every summer, but we

2. (A) do
   (B) doing
   (C) done
   (D) don't

are already ________ about making some changes for next year. Betty says that

3. (A) think
   (B) thinking
   (C) thought
   (D) thoughtful

the French Alps are good for hiking.

5 Keywords

Match each word with its Japanese equivalent.

1. armpit	( )	2. ridge	( )
3. contortion	( )	4. pinch	( )
5. abandon	( )	6. headroom	( )
7. convenient	( )	8. transport	( )
9. alarmingly	( )	10. lift	( )

a. ねじれ	b. エレベーター	c. 頭上スペース	d. 便利な	e. 驚くほど
f. 見捨てる	g. 尾根	h. 脇（わき）	i. 交通	j. 締め付ける

Teatime

イギリスの警察官の身長

- 20 世紀中頃まで警察官は 178cm の身長が求められました。1960 年に男性が 173cm、女性が 163cm に引き下げられましたが、それでも 1990 年代初頭まで 178cm を身長の基準（standard height）にしていたところもありました。その後基準は徐々に撤廃され、今日のイギリスでは、警察官の採用に身長制限（height restriction）はありません。
- 2010 年に勤務わずか 1 か月で逮捕 17 件 という記録を作った警察官の身長は 152cm で、小柄で高性能なことから "laptop"（ノートパソコン）というニックネームがつけられました。"I have martial arts training so I don't see myself as more at risk than any other police officer."（格闘技のトレーニングをしているので、他の警察官より危険なことにはならない）と言っています。

Lesson 2 Seasons

nouns, pronouns, articles

Photographs

Describe the picture by filling in the blanks in these sentences.

1. Some people are (s   ) side by side on the grass.
2. The park is (l   ) and is not very crowded.

1 Reading

05

[1] When someone tells me that Japan is special because it has four seasons, I am never quite sure how to respond. Perhaps one day when I have heard that comment once too many times, I might reply that Hokkaido's summer doesn't last more than a week, and that Okinawa has no time for winter. But I wonder why Japanese people are so concerned with only four seasons? Japan actually has all kinds of seasons: the entrance exam season, the job hunting season, the cherry blossom season, the rainy season, to name just a few.

[2] But yes, the seasons here are very distinct and very powerful. The summer heat can kill people if they aren't careful. In winter, the mountains lure many people to their deaths when blue skies suddenly give way to winter storms. And the typhoon season doesn't need any explanation from me!

[3] England, on the other hand, takes its time to change seasons. We never know for sure when winter ends and spring begins. Seasons in England seem to be integrated, so we can experience two or three seasons in a single day. You can be freezing cold in the morning but sweating at lunchtime, and then drenched to the skin in the afternoon. If this idea could be marketed successfully, we could have visitors coming to England to experience a whole year's worth of weather in just one week.

[4] Now ... just between you and me, seasons actually depress me. When I was a little kid, I loved summer since there was no school and I could play outside in the evening sunshine until late. It was like a dream: I couldn't believe that summer would ever end. When my parents told me I had to go back to school and start going to bed earlier, it was as if the world had ended.

[5] Now I am much older, and a professor who is supposed to be intelligent, and even a little wise. But I am still haunted by the changing seasons. At the end of March, I take the ski rack off my car and change from winter to summer tyres. And then I sit for some time trying to come to grips with the fact that my season for fun has ended and it's time to get back to work.

Notes job hunting「就職活動」 give way to「〜に取って代わる」 take one's time「ゆっくりしている」 between you and me「ここだけの話ですが」 ski rack「スキーラック」 come to grips with「〜を把握する」

A Vocabulary

Find the words in the reading that match these definitions. Write the verbs in their base forms.

1. __________ to answer or respond (line 3)
2. __________ involved in something or affected by it (line 4)
3. __________ to tempt someone to do something (line 8)
4. __________ to connect or combine two or more things (line 12)
5. __________ to make someone feel very sad (line 17)

B Comprehension

Match the beginning of each sentence (1-5) to its ending (a-e) below. Then write the number of the paragraph where the information is found.

1. Japan's seasons are distinctive ______ par. [ ]
2. Even though I have become older and smarter, ______ par. [ ]
3. I am tired of people saying Japan has four seasons ______ par. [ ]
4. When I was a kid, I could never accept ______ par. [ ]
5. Because England's seasons aren't so distinct, ______ par. [ ]

(a) and sometimes quite dangerous.
(b) because I think there are a lot more.
(c) I still feel depressed when my favourite season ends.
(d) that summer would come to an end.
(e) tourists might encounter all the seasons in only one week.

2 Conversation

(A) As you listen to the conversation, fill in the blanks. 06

Dave: They say that winters are becoming warmer. Do you think so?
Elsa: I don't always believe what the news says. This winter was a 1( ).
Dave: Well maybe ... but on TV, they said it was 2( ) to global warming.
Elsa: It's 3( ) to be spring, but it's not warm at all, and I'm still using my 4( ) all day. What's the forecast for tomorrow?
Dave: 5( ) again ... and probably with snow showers.

(B) Listen and fill in the blanks in each question. Then choose the best answer. 07

1. __________ __________ the woman always __________?
   (A) Her friend Dave's ideas. (B) That it is spring.
   (C) That the winter has come. (D) The weather forecast.

2. __________ __________ __________ weather forecast __________?
   (A) It might snow. (B) It will be warm.
   (C) It will freeze. (D) They will have rain showers.

Grammar Points: 名詞、代名詞、冠詞

1. 名詞：数えられる名詞、数えられない名詞

I have to take a taxi, because I have three suitcases.
（スーツケースが 3 個あるので、タクシーに乗らないといけません）

You can walk if you don't have much luggage.（荷物があまりないなら歩けます）

数えられる名詞：bag, suitcase, desk, chair, closet, document, report, etc. 数えられない名詞：luggage, equipment, furniture, advice, information, etc.

2. 代名詞：名詞の性別や人称に一致

Paul always cleans his room by himself.（ポールはいつも自分の部屋を自分で掃除します）

Everybody has to submit their own report by themselves.
（みんな自分のレポートを自分で提出しなければいけません）
* every は単数扱いだが、代名詞は they

3. 冠詞：不特定な名詞につける **a/an**、特定できる名詞につける **the**

Jane had a dog but it is missing now.
（ジェーンは犬を飼っていましたが、今は行方不明になっています）

I suspect the dog I saw in the park is Jane's dog.
（公園で見た犬がジェーンの犬ではないかと思います）

3 Incomplete Sentences

Choose the correct word or phrase to complete each sentence.

1. It is a good idea to wear ________________ when you go out on hot summer days.
   (A) a hat (B) hat (C) its (D) their

2. I lost my sunglasses. Do you know where ________________?
   (A) that is (B) is it (C) them are (D) they are

3. I want ________________ about the weather in England.
   (A) an information (B) several information
   (C) informations (D) some information

4. I forgot to bring my umbrella. Can I borrow ________________?
   (A) your (B) your one (C) yours (D) some of you

5. I think this is ________________ you are looking for.
   (A) a coat (B) the coat (C) that (D) which

4 Text Completion

Select the best answers to complete the text.

Here is the weather forecast for the Midlands and the South. ________ will be a

1. (A) Here
   (B) It
   (C) Those
   (D) Weather

cold start to the day in the Midlands and up in the hills, but ________ temperature

2. (A) a
   (B) high
   (C) the
   (D) your

will rise to a high of 20°C at midday. This will be different in the South. There, it will be a warm and fine morning, but there is a ________ of rain showers here and

3. (A) possible
   (B) possibly
   (C) possibilist
   (D) possibility

there in the late afternoon.

5 Keywords

Match each word or phrase with its Japanese equivalent.

1. tempt	( )	2. freezing	( )
3. intelligent	( )	4. haunt	( )
5. rain shower	( )	6. drench	( )
7. distinct	( )	8. market	( )
9. explanation	( )	10. encounter	( )

a. ～に会う	b. にわか雨	c. 聡明な	d. ～をずぶぬれにする	e. 説明
f. はっきりした	g. ～を誘い込む	h. 絶えずつきまとう	i. 凍るような	j. 市場に出す

Teatime

1日の中に四季

- イギリス人は天気に関し、伝統的な固定観念に取りつかれています。変わりやすい天気（changeable weather conditions）は、“We've seen four seasons in a day.”（1日の中に四季がある）と言います。これはもちろん誇張ですが、季節を問わず天気は変わりやすく、ついさっきまで青空が広がっていたかと思うと、突然雨が降り出します。
- 10分ごとに晴れたり、曇ったり、雨が降ったりの繰り返しということもあり、“If you don't like the weather, just wait for ten minutes.”（その天気が嫌いなら10分待ちなさい）と言うくらいです。そのような天気の変化は、日々の話題を提供してくれます。“When you run out of a topic, talk about the weather.”（話が尽きたら天気のことを話しなさい）と言い、天気をきっかけに会話が弾むのです。

Lesson 3 Be careful with your licence.

auxiliary verbs

Photographs

Describe the picture by filling in the blanks in these sentences.

1. A man is holding a small piece of (p   ) in his right hand.
2. The man looks like a (m   ) of the car park staff.

1 Reading

08

[1] What does your driving licence mean to you? For one thing, I guess, it shows you have spent a lot of time and money at a driving school. And it is probably proof that you have learnt what all those buttons and levers in your car and on your dashboard can do. If you press the right button, your car will become warmer in winter and cooler in summer. Push this button and you can see the road in the dark. Pressing that one and the engine starts.

[2] Your licence also shows that you can drive safely, and I am sure that that is very important. But here in Japan you have to be very careful about your licence. It isn't just a piece of plastic. It really is powerful, and if you abuse it, you could find yourself on the wrong side of the law.

[3] A few years ago I committed an unforgivable crime. I was two days late to renew my licence! At the licensing office, as punishment, I had to explain and apologise and attend driving safety classes all day. The instructor made sure that he targeted me as the bad guy in his class. It wasn't as if I had been caught driving over the speed limit or causing an accident. I was a criminal because of 48 lost hours.

[4] My English driving licence is like a magnificent piece of history. It is very old. It is a large sheet of green paper, folded into many squares, very dirty and dog-eared. To read the information on the document, you have to have excellent eyesight. It's what we call fine print—very fine.

[5] Believe it or not, this antique curiosity is still valid despite two new versions that have come out since I got my licence. The new ones, of course, look like plastic credit cards. I don't have to renew my licence until I am 70 years old, which means that the licence will last for 47 years. British drivers are fortunate that they don't have to keep their licence in their pocket when they drive. If there is a roadside check, drivers can take their licence to their local police station within a week or so. Maybe that relaxed British approach to a licence was the cause of my dilemma in Japan. Maybe I was too relaxed, too.

Notes on the wrong side of the law「違法行為をして」 dog-eared「角が折れた」 curiosity「珍しいもの」 despite「〜にもかかわらず」

A Vocabulary

Find the words in the reading that match these definitions. Write the verbs and nouns in their base forms.

1. ______________ evidence establishing a fact (line 2)
2. ______________ to use something for a bad purpose (line 8)
3. ______________ legally acceptable (line 19)
4. ______________ to remain usable for a specified length of time (line 21)
5. ______________ relating to a particular area (line 24)

B Comprehension

Rearrange the words in brackets to complete each sentence. Then write the number of the paragraph where the information is found.

1. Your licence is proof that you are a safe driver, but don't (after / forget / look / to / your) licence carefully.
   ______________________________________ par. [ ]
2. My old-style licence is good until I am 70, and I (carry / it / me / needn't / with).
   ______________________________________ par. [ ]
3. I was treated badly (I / late / renew / to / was / when) my licence.
   ______________________________________ par. [ ]
4. Your driving licence (that / understand / proves / what / you) the many buttons and levers in your car are for.
   ______________________________________ par. [ ]
5. My English driving licence is a dirty old piece of (information / it / on / paper / with) that is difficult to read.
   ______________________________________ par. [ ]

2 Conversation

(A) As you listen to the conversation, fill in the blanks. 09

son: Hey, Mum. Can you give me a 1( ) to the station, please?
mother: What's wrong with going by 2( )?
son: It's just gone, and I'll be 3( ) if I wait for the next one.
mother: Oh, all right. 4( ) are you going?
son: Into town. I'm meeting Mick, and we're going to 5( ) out some new mobile phones.

(B) Listen and fill in the blanks in each question. Then choose the best answer. 10

1. ________ ________ he ________ ____ ________ to the station?
   (A) He is late. (B) His car is broken.
   (C) It's raining. (D) The car is cheaper.

2. ________ ______ he going to ________ in town?
   (A) He is going to buy a phone. (B) He is going to phone Mick.
   (C) He will go drinking. (D) He will look at some new phones.

Grammar Points: 助動詞

1. can：能力・許可・可能性
   She can speak English well.（彼女は上手に英語を話すことができます）
   Can I watch TV?（テレビを見てもいいですか）
   His story can't be true.（彼の話が本当のはずがありません）

2. will：未来・意志・習性
   I will leave for Australia next week.（来週オーストラリアへ出発します）
   I will be there soon, so please wait for me.（すぐそこに行くので、待っていてください）
   Accidents will happen.（事故は起こるものです）

3. should：義務・必然性（have＋過去分詞）「～すべきだった」
   Who should we vote for?（私たちは誰に投票すべきでしょうか）
   He should be able to give you some good advice.
   （彼なら何かいいアドバイスをくれるはずです）
   You should have spoken more slowly in your speech.
   （スピーチではもっとゆっくり話すべきでした）

4. may：許可・可能性・祈願
   May I smoke?（タバコを吸ってもよろしいですか）
   It may rain this afternoon.（今日の午後、雨が降るかもしれません）
   May you two have a wonderful life!（あなたたち 2 人がすばらしい人生を送れますように）

5. must：義務・確信
   I must wake up early tomorrow.（明日は早起きしなければなりません）
   You must be joking.（あなたは冗談を言っているに違いありません）

3 Incomplete Sentences

Choose the correct word or phrase to complete each sentence.

1. Last week, I ________________ my driving licence.
   (A) can get　(B) can't get　(C) could get　(D) get

2. You have to be careful with your licence because it ________________.
   (A) abuses　(B) abused　(C) can abuse　(D) can be abused

3. I ________________ my driving licence two days ago.
   (A) can renew　(B) will renew　(C) should renew　(D) should have renewed

4. I explained why I was late to renew my licence, but nobody ________________ listen to me.
   (A) could　(B) should　(C) will　(D) would

5. My licence ________________ valid for more than 40 years from now.
   (A) should have been　(B) was
   (C) will be　(D) would

4 Text Completion

Select the best answers to complete the text.

When _____________ you last go to your dentist? When _____________ you need

1. (A) can
   (B) did
   (C) have
   (D) will

2. (A) could
   (B) did
   (C) must
   (D) will

to have your next health check? Although I own a couple of computers and several other pieces of amazing technology, I _____________ seldom come up with the answers to

3. (A) can
   (B) can't
   (C) don't
   (D) never

such everyday questions right away. I have to sit down and slowly read through my old diaries to remember what happened. So I wonder: Did I really need to buy all that technology?

5 Keywords

Match each word or phrase with the Japanese equivalent.

1. eyesight	(　　)	2. unforgivable	(　　)
3. health check	(　　)	4. commit	(　　)
5. come up with	(　　)	6. document	(　　)
7. treat	(　　)	8. check out	(　　)
9. cause	(　　)	10. give ... a lift	(　　)

a. 健康診断	b. 書類	c. 原因	d. 許せない	e. ～を車に乗せる
f. ～を思いつく	g. ～を見てみる	h. 扱う	i. 視力	j. ～を犯す

Teatime

イギリスで車を運転

- イギリスの交通規則は基本的に日本と同じです。車は左側通行なので運転が容易です。イギリス滞在が1年未満であれば、国際運転免許証（International Driving Permit）か日本の運転免許証で運転できます。ただし、レンタカーを借りるときには翻訳証明書を求められることがありますので、国際運転免許証を取得しておいた方が無難です。1年以上の滞在の場合は、英国運転免許証への切り替えが必要となります。
- 英国 DVLA（Driver and Vehicle Licensing Agency）か、DVA（Driver and Vehicle Agency）で英国運転免許証の申請を行うことができます。イギリスではタバコやお酒を買ったり、パブに入ったりする時に、ID の提示が要求されることがあります。そんなときは、英国運転免許証があれば安心です。

Lesson 4 Doctors

to-infinitives, gerunds

Photographs

Describe the picture by filling in the blanks in these sentences.

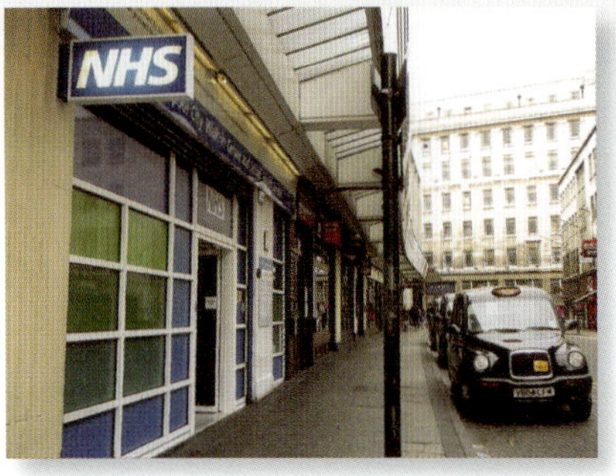

1. This is the (e   ) to the NHS hospital.
2. Taxies are (p   ) along the pavement.

1 Reading

11

[1] I'm sorry to say that I don't have a good opinion of English doctors. Well, that is not exactly true. You see, it's the system that I don't like, not the people who work in it. The National Health Service (NHS) in Britain is a wonderful idea that gives medical care to all people free, or at least quite cheaply.

[2] The problem is that the system has logjams. Patients have to wait hours to receive a short consultation with the doctor, and then they have to put up with another long wait to get their medicine. If they need treatment, their waiting period might extend for weeks, months, or even years. It sounds like a story by Franz Kafka, doesn't it?

[3] The NHS problem is compounded by the local family doctor system. You are only allowed to see one GP, who you have to register with. If that doctor is unable to solve your problem, he or she might tell you to go to a specialist at a hospital, or tell you to come back again—and again.

[4] A good friend of mine had had backache for a long time. She even found it difficult to walk, which came as a shock to her since she had always been a very active person. The doctor prescribed a cream and some painkillers. After a couple of years with no improvement to her condition, she eventually had MRI scans that revealed that she had a degenerative hip joint. Needless to say, she had to wait another year for her hip-replacement operation. Since her problem was not life-threatening, she was at the bottom of the waiting list. Today she is mobile once again, and much happier, but she regrets having wasted all those years waiting.

[5] Japan has a much different approach to treatment. Here, you can choose which local doctor you want to see, which means that you can pick out a specialist for your ailment. Your local clinic most likely has beds where patients can begin receiving treatment. You can have X-rays, injections, drips, blood tests, and rehabilitation all under the same roof. All of this makes the local clinic similar to a convenience store—but for medical complaints.

Notes logjam「行き詰まり」put up with「～に耐える」Franz Kafka「フランツ・カフカ」(1883-1924)。チェコ出身のドイツ語作家。小説『城』は、いつまでたっても城に入れない人を描く。 family doctor「かかりつけの医者」GP (=General Practitioner)「総合診療医」life-threatening「生命に関わるような」

A Vocabulary

Find the words in the reading that match these definitions. Write the verbs and nouns in their base forms.

1. ____________ a meeting with specialists to get their advice (line 6)
2. ____________ to make something worse (line 9)
3. ____________ to recommend the use of a medicine or treatment (line 15)
4. ____________ to make something concealed known (line 16)
5. ____________ a physical or mental disorder (line 22)

B Comprehension

Complete each sentence with a word from the box. Then write the number of the paragraph where the information is found.

choice	free	receive	slow	treatment

1. The NHS system seems to be much too (   ). par. [   ]
2. Patients don't have a (   ) of doctors. par. [   ]
3. In Japan, you can choose your doctor and start your (   ) straight away. par. [   ]
4. The author has mixed feelings about the NHS even though it provides (   ) medical care to many people. par. [   ]
5. It took the author's friend several years to (   ) an operation to replace her damaged hip joint. par. [   ]

2 Conversation

(A) As you listen to the conversation, fill in the blanks. 12

doctor: Now then ... tell me what's wrong.

patient: I feel awful. I'm so 1(   ) that I can't walk, and I can't sleep at night, doctor.

doctor: 2(   ) your appetite?

patient: I've got a 3(   ) and headache, so I don't feel like 4(   ).

doctor: It sounds like you've got the flu. There's a lot of it going around. Take these 5(   ) for three days and then come see me again.

(B) Listen and fill in the blanks in each question. Then choose the best answer. 13

1. ______ ______ the patient ______ ______ ______?
   (A) He has a headache and a fever. (B) He has a stomachache.
   (C) He is dizzy. (D) There's no food in the kitchen.

2. ______ is the ______ ______ for the patient?
   (A) Go to bed and keep warm. (B) Take your medicine.
   (C) You should eat more. (D) You've got the flu.

Grammar Points: to 不定詞、動名詞

1. to 不定詞：

・名詞的用法

My dream is to live abroad.（夢は海外に住むことです）

It is important to see different cultures.（さまざまな文化を知ることは大切です）

・形容詞的用法

I am not in the mood to talk to you.（あなたと話す気分ではありません）

There is nothing to worry about.（何も心配することはありません）

・副詞的用法

She is studying hard to become a lawyer.
（彼女は弁護士になるために、一生懸命勉強しています）

I am glad to see you again.（またお会いできてうれしいです）

2. 動名詞：動詞の意味を持ちながら、名詞としての働き

Smoking too much is bad for your health.（タバコの吸い過ぎは健康に良くありません）

Last weekend, I enjoyed climbing a mountain with my friends.
（先週末、友人と山登りを楽しみました）

He is good at remembering people's names.（彼は人の名前を覚えるのが得意です）

3. to 不定詞と動名詞の使いわけ：意味が異なる場合

Don't **forget** to email me.（私にメールするのを忘れないでください）
Did you **forget** emailing me?（私にメールしたことを忘れたのですか）

I **regret** to say that I cannot accept your invitation.
（残念ながら招待はお受けできないと申しあげねばなりません）
I **regret** saying such things to her.（彼女にあんなことを言って後悔しています）

3 Incomplete Sentences

Choose the correct word or phrase to complete each sentence.

1. I don't have a good opinion of English doctors, and my wife is sure ________________ with me.

   (A) agrees (B) agreed (C) agreeing (D) to agree

2. After ________________ for two hours, I finally received a consultation with the doctor.

   (A) to wait (B) wait (C) waited (D) waiting

3. I went to see another doctor ________________ a second opinion.

   (A) and get (B) for get (C) getting (D) to get

4. I am really happy ________________ she has recovered from her illness.

   (A) hear (B) heard (C) to be heard (D) to hear

5. My grandmother needs ________________ her to the local clinic once a month.

   (A) someone to take (B) taking someone
   (C) someone taking (D) to take someone

4 Text Completion

Select the best answers to complete the text.

I am being bullied. The people around me ________________ me that my stomach is too

1. (A) say
   (B) speak
   (C) tell
   (D) talk

big. They say that ________________ less food and walking for an hour twice a week should

2. (A) eat
   (B) ate
   (C) eaten
   (D) eating

bring results. Feeling depressed about this problem, I remembered ________________ for

3. (A) shopped
   (B) shopping
   (C) to shop
   (D) to shopping

clothes on a recent trip to Hawaii and immediately felt much happier. Why? The trousers there come in huge sizes, 4L, 5L ... making my LL size seem almost tiny.

5 Keywords

Match each word or phrase with its Japanese equivalent.

1. dizzy	(　)	2. treatment	(　)
3. fever	(　)	4. result	(　)
5. appetite	(　)	6. flu	(　)
7. register	(　)	8. bully	(　)
9. straight away	(　)	10. medical care	(　)

a. 食欲	b. インフルエンザ	c. 登録する	d. ただちに	e. ～をいじめる
f. 医療	g. 結果	h. 熱	i. めまいがする	j. 治療

Teatime

イギリスの医療

・イギリスへ移住したり、イギリス国内で引越しをしたりすると、まずすべきことは GP への登録です。GP は General Practitioner の略で、その地域住民のホームドクターを指します。国の税金によって運営され、国民に無料で医療を提供する国民保健サービス NHS（National Health Service）があり、その重要な部分を担っているのが GP です。

・NHS で治療を受けるには、まず GP の診察を受け、GP を通じて適当な病院に紹介してもらいます。外国人であっても、長期滞在するときは、居住地域の GP に登録して、無料で診察を受けることができます。

・ただし NHS は現在、慢性的な予算不足と、それに起因する待機患者などの問題を抱え、手術を受けるのに 1 年以上も待たなければならないケースもあります。

Lesson 5 Business Hours

conjunctions, prepositions

Photographs

Describe the picture by filling in the blanks in these sentences.

1. They are using the ATM (o   ) the bank.
2. The woman using the ATM on the right is (w   ) a sleeveless dress.

1 Reading

14

[1] I know I am going back a few years, but I remember when shops in England had a half-day holiday during the week. I also recall that Saturday was an early-closing day and Sunday was a holiday, or holy day, when people were expected to go to church.

[2] When I first came to Japan, as a naive new foreigner, I was expecting Japan to be similar. So on Saturdays I rushed around doing all my shopping in a panic before the stores closed. It came as quite a shock to me to realise that business was booming at the weekends, and that stores were open on Sundays.

[3] Some shops have now gone to the other extreme and are open 24x7x365—that is, 24 hours a day, seven days a week, 365 days a year. I feel sorry for the night shift in those shops. Most British shops open at nine, an hour earlier than in Japan. But they close on time at six even though some customers might still be in the store. Japanese store clerks tend to wait until all the customers have finished their shopping.

[4] In Japan, if you and I have an appointment and I arrive at our meeting point five minutes before time, I think I am early, but you probably think I am late. In England, it would be bad manners if a bride arrived at the church exactly on time. The same applies to guests going to an informal party. But if it's a dinner party, you should be punctual. Trains in Japan run on time, but London's subway timetables are more laid back; all they say is that trains come every ten minutes or so. Business meetings in Britain tend to finish at the arranged time, which means that you have to present your case quickly and efficiently. Japan's meetings drag on and on, sometimes even into the night, and often the decision made is simply in agreement with what the last person to speak has suggested.

[5] I often think that in Japan, keeping strictly to the timetable is more important than the event itself. I once gave a lecture to a large, attentive audience, and at the end the announcer praised me by saying, "Mr O'Brien is a real professional because he finished right on time." He said very little about the content of my speech, however.

Notes go back「～にさかのぼる」 go to the other extreme「正反対の行動をとる」 apply to「～に当てはまる」 lay back「のんびりとする」 drag on「だらだらと続く」

A Vocabulary

Find the words in the reading that match these definitions. Write the verbs and nouns in their base forms.

1. ______________ lacking experience (line 4)
2. ______________ a very strong feeling of anxiety or fear (line 5)
3. ______________ doing things at the agreed time (line 16)
4. ______________ to offer something for consideration (line 19)
5. ______________ paying close attention to something (line 23)

B Comprehension

Match the beginning of each sentence (1–5) to its ending (a–e). Then write the number of the paragraph where the information is found.

1. When I first came to Japan, I was surprised to find ________ par. [ ]
2. People in other countries have different attitudes ________ par. [ ]
3. In England, shops used to close for half a day twice a week, ________ par. [ ]
4. In Japan it is better to stop lecturing on time than ________ par. [ ]
5. Most British shops open at nine and close on time, ________ par. [ ]

(a) and all day on Sunday.
(b) to worry about the content of the speech.
(c) unlike Japanese shops, which open at ten and take their time closing.
(d) that the shops' closing times were different.
(e) towards being on time.

2 Conversation

(A) As you listen to the conversation, fill in the blanks. 15

man: Look, my plane doesn't leave 1( ) three this afternoon. Let's have an early lunch together and 2( ) over the contract again.

secretary: Yes, that's fine with me. What is 3( ) you about the contract?

man: The main points are OK, but I think the delivery date 4( ) give us enough time to double check the machine.

secretary: What do you 5( ) doing?

man: I want to ask them for a two-week extension.

(B) Listen and fill in the blanks in each question. Then choose the best answer. 16

1. Why does the man want ________ ________ ________ now?
   (A) He is hungry.
   (B) He is in a hurry.
   (C) He has some time before his plane leaves.
   (D) He's worried about the secretary.

2. What does the man ________ ________ ________?
   (A) Double check the machine.
   (B) Make the delivery date later.
   (C) Improve the machine.
   (D) Make a completely new contract.

Grammar Points: 接続詞、前置詞

1. 接続詞：語・句・文をつなぐ

I went out of the room and saw Tom.（部屋を出てトムに会いました）

I think that he is totally wrong.（彼は完全に間違っていると思います）

When I came home, my wife was sleeping.（家に帰ったとき、妻は寝ていました）

If John were here, he would help us out.（もしジョンがここにいれば、助けてくれるでしょう）

I was late because I overslept.（寝坊したので遅刻しました）

その他の接続詞
although, as, before, but, or, so, than, till, though, until, while, etc.

2. 前置詞：名詞（句）・動名詞の前に置く

My younger sister lives in Canada.（妹はカナダに住んでいます）

Yesterday, my children cooked dinner for me.
（昨日、子どもたちが私のために夕食を作ってくれました）

No one knows about his leaving the company.（彼が退社したのを誰も知りません）

He didn't sit down during the conversation.（彼は会話のあいだ座りませんでした）

その他の前置詞
above, among, as, between, by, from, into, of, on, over, under, with, etc.

3 Incomplete Sentences

Choose the correct word to complete each sentence.

1. Shops in England have not only a half-day holiday during the week ____________ also an early-closing day on Saturday.

(A) so (B) but (C) if (D) though

2. It was not ____________ I came to Japan that I found out that business was booming at the weekends.

(A) but (B) when (C) while (D) until

3. You should hurry, ____________ the store will be closed.

(A) and (B) or (C) than (D) that

4. We have to wait for the next train ____________ ten minutes.

(A) at (B) by (C) for (D) in

5. His speech is supposed to finish ____________ five o'clock.

(A) by (B) in (C) on (D) until

4 Text Completion

Select the best answers to complete the text.

When we sat down, the waiter brought us the menu, ________________ my friends became

1. (A) and
   (B) despite
   (C) during
   (D) on

excited. They said, “Hey, look at this one here,” because the menu was full of exotic fish dishes. I didn’t get excited at all. I looked for a dish that had no fish. But I couldn’t find any, ________________ I chose a salad. It’s no fun ________________ you have a fish

2. (A) although
   (B) so
   (C) unless
   (D) without

3. (A) for
   (B) then
   (C) throughout
   (D) when

allergy like I do.

5 Keywords

Match each word or phrase with its Japanese equivalent.

1. extension	(　　)	2. contract	(　　)
3. boom	(　　)	4. dish	(　　)
5. allergy	(　　)	6. content	(　　)
7. delivery	(　　)	8. efficiently	(　　)
9. on time	(　　)	10. look over	(　　)

a. アレルギー	b. 効果的に	c. 延長	d. ～に目を通す	e. 内容
f. 契約	g. 活気づく	h. 定刻に	i. 配達	j. 料理

Teatime

パブの営業時間

- イギリスと言えばパブ（pub）を連想するぐらい、中世からの長い伝統があります。そのパブが今、続々と閉店を余儀なくされています。背景には、若者のビール離れに加え、仕事帰りにパブで一杯やるより家で飲む方を好む人が増えてきたという事情があります。
- 伝統的にパブの営業時間は 11:00 ～ 23:00（日曜日は 12:00 ～ 22:30）と法律で決められていましたが、2005 年に規制が緩和され、許可を得たパブは 23 時以降も営業が可能になりました。しかし実際は、23 時以降もオープンしているパブは少なく、昔からの伝統的な時間内で営業しています。例えば、昔ながらのロンドンの雰囲気を満喫出来る人気パブのレッド・ライオン（The Red Lion）の営業時間は、月曜日から土曜日が 11:30 ～ 23:00、日曜日は閉店です。

Lesson 6 Public Holidays

progressives, causative verbs

Photographs

Describe the picture by filling in the blanks in these sentences.

1. There is a circular swimming (p   ).
2. A white (v   ) is parked beside the fence.

1 Reading

17

[1] Not too long ago, an unhappy worker in a British company took his dispute to court. He explained to the judge that his company had phoned him several times during his summer holiday and asked him to make some business decisions. The man claimed that his holiday had been disrupted, and thus could no longer call it a holiday. The judge listened carefully, considered both sides of the argument, and in the end agreed with the worker. He ordered the worker to begin his holiday once again.

[2] I live and work in Japan, and my holidays are regularly punctuated with phone calls and requests for me to call in at the office. According to the above judgement, then, I've never had a true holiday.

[3] How long should a holiday be? In Japan, having Saturday, Sunday, and Monday off is classified as a three-day holiday. But the British call it a long weekend since they have only gained one extra day. The British talk about having a fortnight in Spain, while the Japanese say we had a nice day trip to Kyoto. Most French workers take a month's summer vacation, which means that their company has to close for all that time.

[4] Do you remember when a few years ago the Japanese car industry was going through a bad time and there was not too much work in the factories? Management's solution was to give the workers an extended holiday for ten days. It was a great idea, but the workers could not relax at all. They were worried that other workers might be taking over their jobs in their absence.

[5] I must admit though, that the Japanese have improved with regard to how to use their free time. Take a look at all the new gardening and DIY shops. This is a good indication that even businessmen who are "married to" their companies are starting to change into casual clothes at the weekends and are growing flowers or fixing things around the house. The British, meanwhile, still regard their holiday time as more important than anything else. How do I know? They still book their vacations a whole year in advance.

Notes take one's dispute to court「法廷闘争に持ち込む」 fortnight「2 週間」 go through「～を経験する」 take over「引き継ぐ」 with regard to「～に関しては」 DIY shop（DIY = do it yourself）「ホームセンター」

A Vocabulary

Find the words in the reading that match these definitions. Write the verbs and nouns in their base forms.

1. ________________ to interrupt or impede the progress of something (line 4)
2. ________________ to arrange or categorise according to characteristics (line 11)
3. ________________ more than what is usual (line 12)
4. ________________ a means of dealing with a difficult situation (line 16)
5. ________________ to become better (line 20)

B Comprehension

Rearrange the words in brackets to complete each sentence. Then write the number of the paragraph where the information is found.

1. The car workers' holiday was too long, (and / couldn't / relax / so / they) enjoy their free time.

   ____ par. [ ]

2. The British judge said that the worker's holiday (been / disrupted / by / had / the) company's phoning him.

   ____ par. [ ]

3. The length (a / according / changes / of / holiday) to the country.

   ____ par. [ ]

4. According to the British judge's decision, (have / holidays / of / none / my) been real holidays.

   ____ par. [ ]

5. Japanese workers (to / are / getting / spending / used) their free time gardening or doing house repairs.

   ____ par. [ ]

2 Conversation

(A) As you listen to the conversation, fill in the blanks. 18

Patrick: We've 1( ) for ten days on holiday in Spain from the 2( ) of August.

Brenda: 3( ) are you going there?

Patrick: We'd thought about driving, but then decided to 4( ) on a package tour.

Brenda: Lucky you. I've got to stay at 5( ) and look after my mother.

(B) Listen and fill in the blanks in each question. Then choose the best answer. 19

1. ________ ________ Patrick going ________ ________?

   (A) For ten days. (B) Early in August.
   (C) From 10th August. (D) Until August.

2. ________ ________ ________ holiday is Patrick going ________ ________?

   (A) He is taking a package tour. (B) He wants to drive around.
   (C) He will hire a car in Spain. (D) He will look after his mother.

Grammar Points: 進行形、使役動詞

1. 進行形

・進行中の動作

I am listening to the radio.（ラジオを聴いています）

He is talking to the client on the phone.（彼は顧客と電話で話しています）

When she called me, I was eating breakfast.
（彼女が電話してきたとき、私は朝食を食べていました）

Jack was talking to someone in the hall.（ジャックが廊下で誰かと話していました）

Who will be making a speech at the conference next week?
（誰が来週の会議でスピーチをするでしょうか）

・変化の途中

My baby is getting bigger day by day.（赤ちゃんは日に日に大きくなっています）

The car was pulling up at a red light.（車が赤信号で停止しようとしていました）

・近い未来の予定

I am starting a new business next month.（来月に新しい仕事を始める予定です）

She was coming back from Paris yesterday, but the flight was canceled.
（彼女は昨日パリから帰ってくる予定でしたが、その便は欠航になりました）

2. 使役動詞

He always makes me laugh.（彼はいつも私を笑わせます）

I will have him call you back as soon as he returns.
（彼が戻り次第、折り返し電話させます）

Let me explain what happened.（何が起こったか、説明させてください）

3 Incomplete Sentences

Choose the correct word or phrase to complete each sentence.

1. The court decision made the company ________________ the worker another holiday.
   (A) gave (B) give (C) given (D) to give

2. Phones were ________________ at my office all day.
   (A) be ringing (B) rang (C) ring (D) ringing

3. We have a two-week holiday, so we ________________ for Spain next week.
   (A) are leaving (B) leaving (C) left (D) were leaving

4. No worker wanted to let someone else ________________ his or her job.
   (A) take over (B) taking over (C) to take over (D) took over

5. Things are ________________ around the house right now.
   (A) be fixing (B) being fixed (C) fix (D) fixing

4 Text Completion

Select the best answers to complete the text.

When I was 15 years old, I was always ________ of becoming a rock star.

1. (A) dream
   (B) dreamed
   (C) dreaming
   (D) dreams

So I had ________ my hair grow down to my shoulders. Father made me

2. (A) allow
   (B) caused
   (C) got
   (D) let

________ it cut short for my older sister's wedding. But a few months later,

3. (A) force
   (B) get
   (C) let
   (D) make

my hair was down to my shoulders again.

5 Keywords

Match each word or phrase with its Japanese equivalent.

1. management	( )	2. take over	( )
3. indication	( )	4. judgement	( )
5. dispute	( )	6. hire	( )
7. book (v)	( )	8. in advance	( )
9. Lucky you.	( )	10. look after	( )

a. 指示　b. 論争　c. 予約する　d. 経営者側　e. ついてるね
f. 前もって　g. ～を引き継ぐ　h. ～を借りる　i. ～の世話をする　j. 判断

Teatime

イギリスの祝祭日

- 祝祭日は英語で public holiday とか national holiday とか言いますが、イギリスでは、銀行をはじめ、オフィスが休みになることから Bank Holiday（バンクホリデー）と呼ばれています。バンクホリデーは月曜日になります。スーパー、デパート、レストランなどは祝祭日もオープンしていますが、営業時間は短くなります。
- 大型連休は春のイースターと冬のクリスマスで、1 年に 8 日の祝祭日があります。New Year's Day（1 月 1 日）、Good Friday（3 月か 4 月）、Easter Monday（3 月か 4 月）、Early May Bank Holiday（5 月第 1 週目の月曜日）、Spring Bank Holiday（5 月最終週の月曜日）、Summer Bank Holiday（8 月の最終週の月曜日）、Christmas Day（12 月 25 日）、Boxing Day（12 月 26 日）。祝祭日は少ないですが、週休 2 日制で有給休暇制度が徹底しているので、結果的には多くの休みを取っています。

Lesson 7 Your Transport, My Transport

adjectives, adverbs

Photographs

Describe the picture by filling in the blanks in these sentences.

1. They are waiting at the bus (s   ).
2. This bus is a double-decker and (n   ) 184.

1 Reading

20

[1] If I were to ask you, "What things are most important for you in your daily life in Japan?" I am sure you would include trains and stations and probably buses as well. It would be hard for you to imagine life without trains. How would you go to school, get to the office, and go shopping? Even if you drive, your car would provide only half an answer.

[2] In London subway trains are essential, though in most other places, people drive to work. England built the world's first railways, but it has been one of the slowest to develop a better system. Margaret Thatcher, who was the Prime Minister of Britain from 1979 to 1990, disliked trains, but, I guess, liked cars, so today Britain has an excellent road network.

[3] Japan's trains famously run on time. Passengers taking part in British transport polls consistently say their trains are usually late. In Japan, when your train comes and it is full, you probably nevertheless squeeze on and stand uncomfortably until you reach your destination. In contrast, the English want to sit during their journey. That is why there are usually more seats on British trains and buses than there are in Japan's commuter trains.

[4] In the past there were two fatal train accidents. A Japanese train ran off the rails on a tight corner and slammed into a concrete building, killing many passengers. An English express did the same. The Japanese driver was evidently speeding to make up a delay of only a couple of minutes. The English crash was caused by inadequate maintenance. One crash concerned time, and the other was about money.

[5] Japan has made many advances in its Shinkansen system and has announced that it will soon start to build a MAGLEV line from Tokyo to Nagoya. But there are still some problems that never seem to go away. Of the 30,000 suicides committed annually in Japan, many occur when people jump in front of trains. So it can be said that trains offer people a way of killing themselves. Another problem that disturbs me is the number of gropers who interfere with women in the trains. Railway companies have admitted defeat in trying to change people's manners, and now have separate cars for women. When it comes to rail transport, Japan seems to have the best and the worst.

Notes Margaret Thatcher「マーガレット・サッチャー」(1925-2013) road network「道路網」 make up「～を取り戻す」 MAGLEV (=magnetic levitation)「リニアモーターカー」 groper「痴漢」

A Vocabulary

Find the words in the reading that match these definitions. Write the verbs and nouns in their base forms.

1. ________________ to give or supply (line 4)
2. ________________ to get into a narrow space (line 11)
3. ________________ the place to which someone is going (line 12)
4. ________________ improvement or progress (line 19)
5. ________________ to make someone feel upset or worried (line 23)

B Comprehension

Complete each sentence with a word from the box. Then write the number of the paragraph where the information is found.

highly	similar	standing	why	without

1. The two crashes were (   ), but the causes were quite different. par. [   ]
2. People can't do (   ) trains in Japan. par. [   ]
3. Because their trains run on time, the Japanese don't mind (   ) in crowded carriages. par. [   ]
4. There was a prime minister of Britain who liked cars, and that's (   ) Britain's road system is so good. par. [   ]
5. Even though Japan has (   ) developed trains like the Shinkansen and the MAGLEV, passengers' behaviour has not improved much. par. [   ]

2 Conversation

(A) As you listen to the conversation, fill in the blanks. 21

Joan: I heard you come by train. Which 1(   ) do you come?

Steve: My wife runs me to Claymore Station, and I get the 7:45 2(   ). I change at Northfield to the local line, ride that for 15 3(   ), and I get to Burstall at ten to nine.

Joan: Are the trains always on 4(   )?

Steve: Yes ... more or less. But if there's a delay, I work through my 5(   ) break to make up.

Joan: Wow! I didn't know you were so dedicated.

(B) Listen and fill in the blanks in each question. Then choose the best answer. 22

1. ____________ ____________ he come ____________ ____________?

(A) His wife drives him. (B) He comes by car.
(C) He takes two trains. (D) He comes by car and two trains.

2. ____________ ____________ if he ____________ ____________?

(A) He apologises. (B) He stays late at night.
(C) He works during his midday break. (D) The boss doesn't mind.

Grammar Points: 形容詞、副詞

1. 形容詞

・限定用法

Hideki Yukawa was the first Japanese to win a Nobel Prize.
(湯川秀樹は、ノーベル賞を受賞した最初の日本人でした)

Everybody appreciates his excellent work.（みんなは彼の優れた仕事を高く評価しています）

She knows how to travel on a tight budget.（彼女は少ない予算で旅する方法を心得ています）

・叙述用法

Are you sure we can trust him?（本当に彼を信用できると思いますか）

If you want to succeed, patience is essential.（成功したいなら、忍耐が必須です）

・限定用法と叙述用法で異なる意味

You should check the website to get the latest information.
(最新の情報を得るために、ウェブサイトをチェックするべきです)

Sorry I'm late.（遅れて申し訳ありません）

2. 副詞

・動詞を修飾

Everyone was listening comfortably to what I was saying.
(みんなは私の言っていることを心地良く聞いていました)

The orchestra has a concert annually.（そのオーケストラは、毎年恒例のコンサートを開催します）

・形容詞・他の副詞を修飾

She is a very intelligent woman.（彼女はとても知的な女性です）

His answers are usually wrong.（彼の答えはたいてい間違っています）

・文全体を修飾（文中・文頭に用いて）

What they are doing is probably illegal.（彼らがやっていることは、おそらく違法です）

Luckily, I was hired right away.（幸運にも、すぐに採用されました）

3 Incomplete Sentences

Choose the correct word or phrase to complete each sentence.

1. There are ________ people who never use the public transportation system.
   (A) few (B) a little (C) less (D) least

2. The excellent British road network will be ________ to you.
   (A) to surprise (B) surprising (C) surprised (D) surprisingly

3. I don't think Britain's commuter system and that of Japan are ________.
   (A) alike (B) like (C) likeliness (D) likely

4. If the train had been ________, the accident would have been prevented.
   (A) proper maintained (B) proper maintenance
   (C) properly maintained (D) properly maintenance

5. I was ________ to learn how many people kill themselves by jumping in front of trains.
   (A) shock (B) shocked (C) shocking (D) shocks

4 Text Completion

Select the best answers to complete the text.

We have a ________________ worker in the office. She is straight out of school and doesn't

1. (A) renew
   (B) new
   (C) newest
   (D) newly

have much confidence in anything she does. She is a very ________________ young woman,

2. (A) nice
   (B) nicer
   (C) nicest
   (D) nicely

but she thinks and speaks too ________________. I hope she can improve in the near future.

3. (A) slow
   (B) slower
   (C) slowest
   (D) slowly

5 Keywords

Match each word or phrase with its Japanese equivalent.

1. local	(　　)	2. confidence	(　　)
3. dedicated	(　　)	4. express	(　　)
5. evidently	(　　)	6. improve	(　　)
7. carriage	(　　)	8. annually	(　　)
9. fatal	(　　)	10. more or less	(　　)

a. 急行	b. 熱心な	c. 良くなる	d. 明らかに	e. 自信
f. 各駅停車の	g. およそ	h. 毎年恒例で	i. 大惨事の	j. 車両

Teatime

便利なロンドンの地下鉄

- ロンドンの地下鉄は underground とか tube（チューブ）と呼ばれ、12 の路線があります。料金はゾーン制（zone system）で、回数券や 1 日乗り放題チケットの Travel Card（トラベルカード）もあります。Zone 1 から Zone 6 の範囲内では Oyster Card（オイスターカード）を購入すると便利です。
- Exact Money Only という表示がある自動券売機は、おつりが出ません。小銭がなければ窓口（ticket office）で購入するとよいです。片道（single）切符は adult single と child single があり、往復（return）切符を買うこともできます。大晦日など特別な行事の時は、改札口が解放され、チケットなしで自由に乗り降りできます。
- 日本と違いイギリスでは、地下鉄の乗り越し精算は認められていません。50 ポンドの罰金（penalty fare）が科せられるので、乗車前に料金を確認してからチケットを購入することが必要です。

Lesson 8 Convenience Stores

perfect tenses (present perfect, past perfect, future perfect)

Photographs

Describe the picture by filling in the blanks in these sentences.

1. The store in the middle is (o   ), but nobody can be seen inside.
2. There are only a few pedestrians on the (p   ).

1 Reading

23

[1] Would you believe that there are about 50,000 convenience stores in Japan? They all offer an amazingly wide range of sophisticated customer services, which, naturally, is why they are called convenience stores. Their main business has been to sell lunches, either in the form of sandwiches or rice balls or lunch boxes. If you often buy your lunch at a convenience store, you don't need to worry about eating the same food day after day. The system takes care of all that, offering a variety of lunches that rotate daily. The boom in this kind of shopping has not yet taken off in Britain, but it will happen before long, I'm sure.

[2] What all this means is that these shops have changed our lifestyles. We no longer have to make our own lunch. Since the stores are everywhere, we don't need to plan where to stop and eat when we go for a drive. We can even do our daily shopping at these stores, or use them as a bank, post office, or delivery centre.

[3] But I am sure that you are aware that this business comes at a price. It really is a cutthroat competition, with the successful shops knocking out the weaker rivals. There is a tiny profit margin on a store's items, and the manager has to fight constantly to generate more profit while cutting costs. The system for ordering goods and delivering them to each shop is pretty high tech and quite stressful. The manager must decide what is going to sell and what isn't. If he is correct every day, the shop stays in business. If he isn't, well, there goes his job. On average, trucks bring various goods to each shop five times a day.

[4] Santa Claus recently brought me a GPS navigation system for my car, and I get a big kick out of looking at the map and road system. The map automatically twists and turns according to the direction in which I am driving.

[5] Little blue, orange, and green symbols appear that tell me which convenience stores are located on which corners. "Look, there it is!" I often say, "We have to turn left here at Lawsons." Yes, these stores have now become our important landmarks that make us feel more at ease in our busy lives.

Notes take off「(ブーム) が起こる」 cutthroat「熾烈な」 profit margin「利幅」 stay in business「営業を継続する」 there goes「～がなくなる」 get a kick out of「～から快感を得る」

A Vocabulary

Find the words in the reading that match these definitions. Write the verbs and nouns in their base forms.

1. ________________ advanced or complicated (line 2)
2. ________________ to take turns or alternate (line 6)
3. ________________ the amount of money spent on running a business (line 15)
4. ________________ something that represents something else (line 22)
5. ________________ a building or feature that is easily noticed (line 24)

B Comprehension

Match the beginning of each sentence (1-5) to its ending (a-e). Then write the number of the paragraph where the information is found.

1. Convenience stores have changed how we live ________ par. [ ]
2. I find it exciting to look at my car's GPS ________ par. [ ]
3. It seems that the status of the stores has changed ________ par. [ ]
4. The store business is very competitive ________ par. [ ]
5. Japan's convenience stores are more advanced than those in Britain ________ par. [ ]

(a) and the managers have a lot of stress.
(b) as it follows where I am driving.
(c) because they can take care of so many of our daily needs.
(d) because they have now become important landmarks for travellers.
(e) since they offer a different choice of lunches each day.

2 Conversation

(A) As you listen to the conversation, fill in the blanks. 24

Jill: What do you usually do for lunch? Do you eat out, or do you 1( ) your own?

Mike: I usually go to the corner shop and 2( ) something, but once in a while I go to a 3( ) restaurant.

Jill: What about today? Do you have any 4( )?

Mike: No, not really. Then shall we go to the Taj Mahal and have a 5( )?

Jill: Great idea! See you at twelve.

(B) Listen and fill in the blanks in each question. Then choose the best answer. 25

1. ________ ________ Mike like to ______ ______ ____________ for a change?
   (A) He brings a lunch box. (B) He eats lunch in the office.
   (C) He goes to a restaurant. (D) He goes to the corner shop.

2. ________ ________ going ________ ____________ today?
   (A) He hasn't decided yet. (B) He will eat alone.
   (C) He will go to the corner shop. (D) He will have a lunch date.

Grammar Points: 完了時制（現在完了、過去完了、未来完了）

1. 現在完了：have + 動詞の過去分詞形

   I have decided what I will study in college.（大学で何を学ぶか決めました）

   I have been to New Zealand twice.（2 度ニュージーランドに行ったことがあります）

   I have known Sara since we were little kids.（小さい子どもの頃からサラを知っています）

2. 過去完了：had + 動詞の過去分詞形

   He had already gone when I got there.（私がそこに到着した時、彼はすでに帰っていました）

   I had never seen Mt. Fuji until a year ago.（1 年前まで富士山を見たことがありませんでした）

   I had worked for a bank for ten years by then.（その時まで 10 年間銀行に勤めていました）

3. 未来完了：will have + 動詞の過去分詞形

   The meeting will have finished by seven pm.（午後 7 時までには会議は終っているでしょう）

   By the time you leave Japan, you will have been asked the same questions many times.
   （あなたが日本を離れるまでには、同じ質問を何度もされることになるでしょう）

   Next year, we will have lived in New York for twenty years.
   （来年で、私たちは 20 年間ニューヨークに住んでいることになります）

3 Incomplete Sentences

Choose the correct word or phrase to complete each sentence.

1. I have never ________________ about my lunch because there are so many convenience stores near the office.

   (A) worried (B) had worried (C) worry (D) worrying

2. Have you ________________ the package I sent you yesterday?

   (A) had received (B) receive (C) received (D) receiving

3. Next month I ________________ the manager of a convenience store for one year.

   (A) had been (B) has been (C) have been (D) will have been

4. The delivery truck ________________ just now.

   (A) arrive (B) had arrived (C) has arrived (D) arriving

5. A new convenience store opened last week where there ________________ a gas station.

   (A) been (B) had been (C) has been (D) is

4 Text Completion

Select the best answers to complete the text.

I've been ________________ here for ten years. Before I graduated from university, I

1. (A) work
   (B) works
   (C) worked
   (D) working

________________ thought it was easy to be a salesman, but now I have changed my point

2. (A) am
   (B) have
   (C) had
   (D) was

of view. Of course you have to understand your product in detail, but you also have to build up the trust of your customers. Over the years I ________________ become a friend

3. (A) am
   (B) have
   (C) has
   (D) having

of my clients, and that is why most of them have not thought about changing to other companies' products.

5 Keywords

Match each word or phrase with its Japanese equivalent.

1. competition	(　　)	2. direction	(　　)
3. automatically	(　　)	4. feel at ease	(　　)
5. on average	(　　)	6. profit	(　　)
7. once in a while	(　　)	8. for a change	(　　)
9. in detail	(　　)	10. point of view	(　　)

a. 安心する	b. 平均して	c. 見方	d. 利益	e. 気分転換に
f. 自動的に	g. 方角	h. 詳しく	i. 時々	j. 競争

Teatime

ロンドンのコーナーショップ

- 日本語の「コンビニ」の語源である convenience store はアメリカ発祥の言葉で、"a shop that is often open 24 hours a day"（24 時間営業の店）と定義されています。イギリスでコンビニに相当する店は corner shop（コーナーショップ）と呼ばれ、"a small shop that sells food, cigarettes, and other things that people need every day"（食べ物、タバコ、その他毎日の生活必需品を売る店）が定義です。
- ロンドンの街中でも 24 時間営業の店は少なく、ほとんどが午後 10 時には閉店します。コーナーショップが提供しているものはコンビニに近く、食べ物や飲み物、お酒、生活雑貨などの他、宝くじ、バスや地下鉄に使うオイスターカード、公共料金の支払いができるサービスや ATM もあります。ただし、お酒のコーナーは、深夜にはカバーが掛けられ買うことができません。

Lesson 9 Is it a good noise?

negatives

Photographs

Describe the picture by filling in the blanks in these sentences.

1. Four men are playing musical (i   ).
2. All of them are wearing (s   ).

1 Reading

26

[1] When you go abroad, you soon start noticing that little things are quite different from your society back home. And so it was with me when I became a teacher in Japan. My classes were full of polite young people, and everything was going well until the students began to catch colds. That was when I felt something was horribly wrong, and that I shouldn't be in this country.

[2] In England when you have a cold, it is most important to blow your nose into a tissue or handkerchief. You should never, never sniff your runny nose back upwards. Some teachers in England completely lose it when a student does this. But, you might say, this is Japan. Here, blowing your nose in public, especially during meals or other formal situations, is taboo, so students sniff, wait a moment, sniff again. I guess the answer is, "When in Rome ...." Other noises triggered a similar reaction in me. Here, for example, noodles and tea are thought to be tastier when they are noisily slurped into the mouth.

[3] Animals' noises soon drove me crazy as well. A rice field at night, full of croaking frogs, and a tree filled with at least a million singing cicadas were beyond belief. The tiny buzz of a nighttime mosquito caused me to lose sleep. I was astonished when some friends told me they bought insects that sounded like bells ringing and kept them in their houses! I was convinced that these people were sick.

[4] My years in Japan have turned most of these bad noises into good ones, and my anger has been diverted to newer complaints. Trains and stations have endless announcements about doors, running, luggage, old people, and so on, but most passengers no longer listen to them. Such announcements have become unwanted noises that we automatically shut out. Meanwhile, TV talk shows don't seem to be able to get along without groups of people whose job it is to laugh loudly and make all kinds of noise. I truly believe that half of my TV licence fee goes towards program content, while the other half is for supporting noise.

[5] The crunch of gravel when you walk through a Japanese garden; the squeak of fresh snow when you ski on it; the breathing of a sleeping baby. These noises usually don't bother me. But loud children in restaurants and talkative middle-aged women in trains still drive me up the wall.

Notes runny nose「鼻水」 lose it「怒る」 When in Rome .... (=When in Rome, do as the Romans do.)「郷に入っては郷に従え」 rice field「水田」 beyond belief「信じられないほどの」 TV licence fee「テレビ受信料」 drive ... up the wall「～をイライラさせる」

A Vocabulary

Find the words in the reading that match these definitions. Write the verbs and nouns in their base forms.

1. ______________ showing consideration or respect for others (line 3)
2. ______________ something that shouldn't be done (line 9)
3. ______________ something felt in response to a situation (line 10)
4. ______________ to change course or turn from one direction to another (line 18)
5. ______________ what a thing is made up of (line 23)

B Comprehension

Rearrange the words in brackets to complete each sentence. Then write the number of the paragraph where the information is found.

1. Unlike in Japan, sniffing is not tolerated in England and (drinks / is / neither / slurping / your).
   ______________________________ par. [ ]
2. Although I (animal / enjoy / have / to / started) noises, I dislike train announcements and talk shows on TV.
   ______________________________ par. [ ]
3. There are some nice (like / noises / or / snow / squeaky) a crunchy gravel path, but kids in restaurants and talkative women in trains are not nice noises.
   ______________________________ par. [ ]
4. When my students started catching colds, I (and / dislike / Japan / started / to) wanted to go home.
   ______________________________ par. [ ]
5. I couldn't stand the noises of insects, and I thought that the (as / kept / people / them / who) pets were strange.
   ______________________________ par. [ ]

2 Conversation

(A) As you listen to the conversation, fill in the blanks. 27

receptionist: Good morning, madam. May I 1( ) you?
guest: I'd like to 2( ) a complaint. My room was so noisy last night that I 3( ) sleep at all.
receptionist: I'm very sorry about that. Let me 4( ) your room.
guest: Thank you very much. I'm 5( ) better already.

(B) Listen and fill in the blanks in each question. Then choose the best answer. 28

1. What was the ____________ ____________ with her room?
   (A) It was dirty. (B) It was too bright.
   (C) It was too noisy. (D) It was too small.

2. What was the ____________ ____________ ____________?
   (A) All the rooms are full. (B) Have a different room.
   (C) Here is your money back. (D) I'll ask the manager.

Grammar Points: 否定

1. 動詞を否定

You don't have to worry about him.（彼の心配をする必要はありません）

I couldn't take my eyes off her.（彼女から目を離すことができませんでした）

I will never forget this as long as I live.（このことは一生忘れません）

2. 名詞を否定

There were no cars in the parking lot.（駐車場には車が 1 台もありませんでした）

That's no way to speak to elder people.
（年上の人にそんな話し方をするものではありません）

No one lives in this house.（この家には誰も住んでいません）

3. 否定の意味を含む副詞

When I came to Japan, I could hardly speak any Japanese.
（日本に来たとき、ほとんど日本語が話せませんでした）

My father rarely drinks alcohol.（父はめったに酒を飲みません）
☞ hardly, scarcely は程度がわずか、rarely, seldom は頻度がわずかであることを表す。

4. 否定の意味を含む形容詞

Few people know about him.（彼のことを知っている人はほとんどいません）

There is little time left.（ほとんど時間は残っていません）

3 Incomplete Sentences

Choose the correct word or phrase to complete each sentence.

1. I ________________ to school because I caught a cold.
(A) couldn't go (B) doesn't go (C) not going (D) not to go

2. I have ________________ people sniff their runny nose in England.
(A) don't see (B) never seen (C) not see (D) see no

3. I ________________ a good night sleep last night because of a mosquito.
(A) didn't have (B) have never (C) have no (D) won't have

4. Our family ________________ TV during meals.
(A) never watching (B) not watching
(C) rarely watch (D) watching no

5. There ________________ footprints on the fresh snow.
(A) has not been (B) isn't a (C) have no (D) were no

4 Text Completion

Select the best answers to complete the text.

I ______________ believe that winter has come again so soon. It seems as if last winter

1. (A) can't
   (B) doesn't
   (C) have
   (D) will

was just the other day and not a whole year away. Autumn ______________ stay long,

2. (A) can't
   (B) didn't
   (C) hasn't
   (D) won't

did it? The maple leaves were beautiful this year, but now the trees look very bare and lonely. I ______________ get out my winter sweaters, and must not forget to tidy the

3. (A) am going
   (B) were going to
   (C) will have to
   (D) will must

garden before it snows.

5 Keywords

Match each word or phrase with the Japanese equivalent.

1. complaint	(　　)	2. maple	(　　)
3. tolerate	(　　)	4. trigger	(　　)
5. bare	(　　)	6. tidy	(　　)
7. gravel	(　　)	8. slurp	(　　)
9. squeaky	(　　)	10. in public	(　　)

a. 引き起こす	b. 砂利	c. 人前で	d. 葉が落ちて	e. 手入れする
f. 不満	g. 大目に見る	h. カエデ	i. 音を立ててすする	j. きしる

Teatime

不快な音

- 日本人は、夏に一斉に鳴くセミの声も、秋の心地よい鈴虫の声も、季節を感じさせる良い音として聞きます。しかしイギリス人には雑音に過ぎません。聞き慣れていない音は不快な音になります。イギリスでは、スープをすする音や食器の接触音、ゲップなどは不快な音で、マナー違反とみなされます。
- イギリス人は、日本人の鼻水をすする（sniff）音も大変いやがります。逆に大きな音をたてて鼻をかむ（blow one's nose）のは OK なのです。日本人は人前では、咳やくしゃみの音を少しでも小さくしようとしますが、イギリス人は大音響で咳やくしゃみをします。
- 良い音と不快な音は、その国の文化や習慣、マナーによって異なりますので、相手に悪い印象を与えないようにしましょう。"When in Rome, do as the Romans do."（郷に入っては郷に従え）です。

Lesson 10 Fireworks

interrogatives, imperatives

Photographs

Describe the picture by filling in the blanks in these sentences.

1. The bonfire is (b   ).
2. It is dark and nobody can be (s   ) around the bonfire.

1 Reading

29

[1] Ask an Englishman what he likes about autumn and he might tell you that Bonfire Night is a fond childhood memory. The tradition is to make a big fire in our garden on the night of 5th November, and to let off fireworks. We also make a life-sized doll—a "guy"—using Dad's old clothes, and then put the guy onto the fire and burn it. It sounds like fun, doesn't it?

[2] We need to know more about this "guy," however. His modern name is Guy Fawkes. In 1605, because Fawkes didn't like the persecution of the Catholics by Queen Elizabeth I and King James I, he decided to make a bomb and explode it in the basement of the Parliament building in London. But he was caught in the act and sentenced to death. So in fact, when we British people enjoy Bonfire Night, we are celebrating something quite horrific.

[3] Japan's fireworks, in contrast, are synonymous with summer. Instead of fireworks warming you up on a cold November night, Japanese fireworks cool you down on a sweltering midsummer evening. Most cities have a local fireworks show with night stalls selling crushed ice, paper fans, greasy food, and anything else that might make a profit.

[4] When the British set off fireworks, they wear winter boots, a thick coat, gloves, and a scarf and woollen hat. For you, this may be hard to imagine since in Japan, fireworks are enjoyed in shorts, sandals, and thin shirts. Wearing a lightweight cotton yukata to a fireworks show not only looks good, but keeps you cool, a good thing when the temperature is still 25°C even at night.

[5] November in Britain is cold, and if you are sneezing or have a runny nose, there's little that cupid can do for you. It's not a good season for romance. In summer in Japan, however, romance has a chance to flourish since we all look more attractive in our festival clothes, especially in a half light. But the morning reveals the reality of the previous night's fun. The river bank has to be cleaned of litter—bottles, cans, leftover food, and paper from the fireworks. Was it worth it? All that money went up in smoke! I think the answer is yes. Because the fireworks last only for an instant, we have to concentrate on them and use our memories to remember what happened. And that is worthwhile.

Notes Bonfire Night「焚き火の夜」 Guy Fawkes「ガイ・フォークス」(1570-1606) Elizabeth I「エリザベス1世」(1533-1603)。在位 1558-1603 James I「ジェームズ1世」(1566-1625)。在位 1603-1625 set off「～を打ち上げる」 half light「薄明り」

A Vocabulary

Find the words in the reading that match these definitions. Write the verbs and nouns in their base forms.

1. ________________ a long-established custom (line 2)
2. ________________ the floor of a building below ground level (line 7)
3. ________________ very hot (line 12)
4. ________________ to develop successfully (line 21)
5. ________________ to focus all one's attention on something (line 25)

B Comprehension

Complete each sentence with a word from the box. Then write the number of the paragraph where the information is found.

called	burn	done	local	watching

1. Japan's fireworks shows are held at night in summer, and are part of a ( ) festival. par. [ ]
2. The British tradition is to make a life-sized doll, and then ( ) it on a fire in the garden. par. [ ]
3. Japan's summer festivals are perhaps more romantic than England's, but there is a lot of clearing-up to be ( ) in the morning. par. [ ]
4. About four hundred years ago, a man ( ) Guy Fawkes planted a bomb in the basement of the Parliament building. par. [ ]
5. In England, you need a lot of clothes to keep warm when ( ) fireworks, but not here in Japan. par. [ ]

2 Conversation

(A) As you listen to the conversation, fill in the blanks. 30

wife: The newspaper says that the city is thinking about having a big fireworks 1( ) in November.

husband: Really? I'm not too 2( ) on that. All that money up in smoke, just for a few minutes of 3( ).

wife: Yeah. It makes 4( ) when you say it like that.

husband: Why don't they save half of the budget, and give it to a good 5( )?

wife: Hey, that's a good idea.

(B) Listen and fill in the blanks in each question. Then choose the best answer. 31

1. Why does the husband ____________ ____________ the ____________ ____________?
   (A) It is a waste of money. (B) November is too cold.
   (C) Summer is a better season. (D) The fireworks make too much smoke.

2. What ____________ ____________ ____________________?
   (A) Change the site. (B) Cut down the scale of the show.
   (C) Donate half of the budget to charity. (D) Give all the money to charity.

Grammar Points: 疑問文、命令文

1. 疑問文

・yes / no で答えられるもの

Are you serious?（本気ですか）

Do you like this town?（この町が好きですか）

Can you tell me your new address?（あなたの新しい住所を教えてくれますか）

・疑問詞を用いたもの

What brought you to Japan?（どうして日本に来たのですか）

Who were you talking to?（誰と話していたのですか）

When was the last time you cleaned your room?（最後に部屋を掃除したのはいつでしたか）

Where do you want me to take you?（どこに連れて行ってほしいですか）

Why did he quit his job?（なぜ彼は仕事を辞めたのですか）

Whose phone is this?（これは誰の電話ですか）

How do you pronounce this word?（この単語はどう発音しますか）

・付加疑問

It's still hot outside, isn't it?（外はまだ暑いですね）

You don't have to go back home right now, do you?（今すぐ家に帰る必要はないですよね）

2. 命令文

Be patient for a while.（しばらくのあいだ我慢してください）

Come to my office right now.（今すぐオフィスに来てください）

Don't talk back to me.（私に口答えしてはいけません）

3 Incomplete Sentences

Choose the correct word or phrase to complete each sentence.

1. ________ clothes are used for this life-sized doll?

(A) How (B) Who (C) Who's (D) Whose

2. ________ is the reason he decided to blow up the building?

(A) How (B) What (C) When (D) Why

3. This city also has a fireworks show, ________?

(A) did it (B) didn't it (C) does it (D) doesn't it

4. ________ taught you how to wear a kimono?

(A) How (B) When (C) Where (D) Who

5. ________ leave any garbage behind.

(A) Didn't (B) Doesn't (C) Don't (D) Isn't

4 Text Completion

Select the best answers to complete the text.

The other day in town, I saw a man who appeared to be lost. He had a big, black daypack on his back, and he was looking at a map. "_______________ you lost? Where do you

1. (A) Can
   (B) Are
   (C) Where
   (D) Why

_______________ to go?" I asked. He said he was looking for the subway to the Shinkansen

2. (A) want
   (B) wanted
   (C) wants
   (D) wanting

station. "That's easy. _______________ down those stairs, and through the ticket barrier,

3. (A) Go
   (B) Goes
   (C) Going
   (D) Went

and the subway train that you want is on the left.

5 Keywords

Match each word or phrase with its Japanese equivalent.

1. site	(　　)	2. worthwhile	(　　)
3. daypack	(　　)	4. fireworks	(　　)
5. life-sized	(　　)	6. donate	(　　)
7. persecution	(　　)	8. budget	(　　)
9. ticket barrier	(　　)	10. let off	(　　)

a. 寄付する	b. 等身大の	c. 場所	d. ～を打ち上げる	e. 価値がある
f. 迫害	g. 改札口	h. 花火	i. デイパック	j. 予算

Teatime

イギリスの花火の季節

- 日本では花火は夏の風物詩ですが、イギリスでは10月末から11月にかけて、各地で花火大会が催されます。これは400年以上も前にガイ・フォークスという人が、11月5日の議会開院式にイギリスの国会議事堂を爆破しようとして捕まり処刑されたことに起因します。これ以降、この時期に花火を打ち上げて国の平和を願うようになりました。
- 11月5日はGuy Fawkes Night（ガイ・フォークス・ナイト）と呼ばれ、伝統的に子供たちが古着や新聞などで作った人形をガイ・フォークスに見立てて街中を引き回し "A penny for the guy!"（ガイ人形に1ペニーください）と言って、通行人から小銭をもらい、夜に人形を燃やしていました。今では一部の地域を除いて、その風習は廃れ、かがり火と花火を楽しむ日になっています。
- ロンドン･アイを中心にテムズ川で打ち上げられる新年を祝う恒例の花火は、その迫力で人気があります。

Lesson 11 Public or Private?

participles (present participle, past participle)

Photographs

Describe the picture by filling in the blanks in these sentences.

1. Four people are sitting (o   ).
2. The man wearing glasses is wearing a short-sleeved (s   ).

1 Reading

32

[1] In Victorian England, women's legs and ankles were hidden from view by long skirts. But nothing lasts forever, especially in fashion, and over time, skirts grew shorter and shorter. In 1964 a young designer named Mary Quant introduced the mini skirt, a piece of clothing that was not for hiding but for revealing. The mini skirt shocked the whole world. After that, it seemed, nothing could ever be private again.

[2] Since the 1960s, most of the unwritten rules about what you can and cannot do in public have been abandoned. Etiquette in Japanese trains has undergone many changes. In the old days, when we had a conversation on the train, we tried to keep it private, but today passengers share their thoughts with everyone. The mobile phone encourages us to make our private conversations public. We talk into the phone in a loud voice, and the whole car can hear us. Shouldn't we be worried about doing that?

[3] Eating and drinking on the train, except in long-distance trains, was never seen in the old days, either. Today, though, that principle has gone. It is not uncommon to see a young woman passenger push food and drink into her mouth and then put cream, lipstick, make-up, and eyelashes on her face. Does she think she is making herself look beautiful?

[4] Everyone seems to be nervous and nobody can sit still and relax anymore. We all have to play with our phones or listen to music and tap our feet. And some of us who are old-fashioned, read books. Are we losing our self-confidence?

[5] Well, books are not so bad. But Japan is still well-known worldwide because its businessmen aren't ashamed to read comics on the train. British railway passengers are loud telephoners, but they still are careful about what they read in public. In Japan recently, it seems that the floor has also changed its function. At home, we have tatami mats that we can walk or sit on and relax, and that makes me happy after a long day at the office. But today, young people like to sit on the floors in trains and stations—and even on the stairs. Is sitting on the floor more comfortable than a bench? Or is it a little protest against heavy social rules?

Notes Victorian「ビクトリア女王時代の」 Mary Quant「マリー・クワント」(1934-)。ファッションデザイナー unwritten rules「暗黙の了解」long-distance train「長距離列車」self-confidence「自信」

A Vocabulary

Find the words in the reading that match these definitions. Write the verbs and nouns in their base forms.

1. ________ to bring something into use for the first time (line 3)
2. ________ to pass through or experience (line 7)
3. ________ to stimulate or spur (line 9)
4. ________ a rule or standard, especially of good behaviour (line 13)
5. ________ the action for which a thing is particularly fitted or used (line 22)

B Comprehension

Match the beginning of each sentence (1–5) to its ending (a-e). Then write the number of the paragraph where you find the information.

1. Train manners have changed, and now young women eat and drink, ________ par. [ ]
2. Fashion always changes and skirts gradually became shorter ________ par. [ ]
3. Businessmen don't worry about reading comics, ________ par. [ ]
4. Conversations in the train used to be private, ________ par. [ ]
5. In the train we are unable to sit quietly, and we have to play ________ par. [ ]

(a) and young people don't mind sitting on the floor.
(b) and then put on make-up.
(c) but mobile phones have made them public.
(d) with mini skirts in the 1960s being the shortest of all.
(e) with something or listen to music.

2 Conversation

(A) As you listen to the conversation, fill in the blanks. 33

David: This is a very nice restaurant, isn't it?

Brenda: Yes, but there's a terrible ${}_{1}$( ). Look at the next table. There's a man smoking a cigarette. Would you ${}_{2}$( ) him to stop?

David: Excuse me, but this is a no-smoking restaurant. Would you ${}_{3}$( ) stopping, please?

Brenda: Ah, thanks, David. That's much ${}_{4}$( ).

David: Well, perhaps we can enjoy our ${}_{5}$( ) now. Are you ready to order? Here's the waiter.

(B) Listen and fill in the blanks in each question. Then choose the best answer. 34

1. ________ ________ the woman ________ ________ in the restaurant?
   (A) Her dinner date was late. (B) Somebody had lit a cigarette.
   (C) It was too noisy. (D) The waiter didn't come.

2. ________ ________ David ________ ________ the smoker?
   (A) Angrily. (B) Jokingly. (C) Politely. (D) Strongly.

Grammar Points: 分詞（現在分詞、過去分詞）

1. 名詞を修飾

Do you know the girl talking with him over there?
（あそこで彼と話している女の子を知っていますか）

The city has a street named after a famous movie star.
（その町は有名な映画スターにちなんで名づけられた通りがあります）

Let sleeping dogs lie.（眠っている犬を寝かしておきなさい / さわらぬ神にたたりなし）

The number of accidents caused by drunken drivers is increasing.
（飲酒運転者によって起こされる事故数が増加しています）

2. 補語

He kept talking in English for an hour.（彼は 1 時間英語で話し続けました）

I left the job unfinished and went to bed.（仕事を終えないまま寝ました）

3. 分詞構文

Speaking of that matter, I have a different idea.
（その問題について言うと、私には違った考えがあります）

Seen from a distance, the building looks like a ship.
（遠くから眺めると、その建物は船のように見えます）

3 Incomplete Sentences

Choose the correct word or phrase to complete each sentence.

1. In Victorian England, it was rare to see women's legs ______________ from their skirts.
   (A) have shown (B) showed (C) showing (D) shows

2. ______________ by mobile phones, people make their conversations public in a place like a train.
   (A) Encourage (B) Encouraged (C) Encouraging (D) To encourage

3. The woman swallowed the food ______________ into her mouth.
   (A) push (B) pushed (C) pushing (D) to push

4. Reading books in the train is becoming ______________.
   (A) outdate (B) outdated (C) outdating (D) to outdate

5. ______________ tatami mats after a long day of work makes me feel relaxed.
   (A) Sat by (B) Sit on (C) Sitting on (D) To sit

4 Text Completion

Select the best answers to complete the text.

_______________ my house, I put my umbrella in my bag. _______________ to the station

1. (A) Leave
   (B) Left
   (C) Leaving
   (D) Leaves

2. (A) Gone
   (B) Went
   (C) Walked
   (D) Walking

I felt pleased knowing that I wouldn't get wet even if it rained. Half an hour later I got off the train and went to the clock tower to meet Jenny. She had already arrived, but she was soaked from head to toe. I looked for my umbrella in my bag. That's when I noticed my umbrella was _______________.

3. (A) miss
   (B) missed
   (C) missing
   (D) to miss

5 Keywords

Match each word or phrase with its Japanese equivalent.

1.	eyelash	(　　)	2.	upset	(　　)
3.	well-known	(　　)	4.	abandon	(　　)
5.	protest	(　　)	6.	jokingly	(　　)
7.	soak	(　　)	8.	swallow	(　　)
9.	uncommon	(　　)	10.	from head to toe	(　　)

a. ～をのみ込む	b. まつげ	c. 反抗	d. ～を捨てる	e. 全身
f. よく知られている	g. ふざけて	h. めずらしい	i. 動転させる	j. ～をずぶぬれにする

Teatime

通勤電車で化粧

- 日本の若い女性が、朝の通勤電車で化粧（makeup）をしているのをよく見かけます。この現象は日本だけでなく、イギリスでも同じです。地下鉄で化粧をするのは図書館でしゃべるのと同じようにタブーとみなされていましたが、ある調査によれば、およそ 3 分の 2（two-thirds）の女性がロンドンの地下鉄で化粧をした経験があるそうです。
- 電車での化粧は批判が多く、容認派が少ないのは事実です。容認派の主張は、電車に乗っている時間を有意義に使うべきで、自分とは無関係の他人だから化粧途中の顔を見られても平気というもの。批判派は、化粧は見えないところでするのが基本で、化粧をしている姿を見せるのはマナー違反だと言います。人前で化粧をするということに関し、新たなマナーの規範が作られつつあるのかもしれません。

Lesson 12 Technology

relatives

Photographs

Describe the picture by filling in the blanks in these sentences.

1. The man appears to be (c   ) something about a car.
2. He is wearing a (c   ) and a high visibility jacket.

1 Reading

35

[1] The car park was in the centre of the famous historical city. I had been warned that it was almost impossible to park your car there, because it was nearly always full. But it must have been my lucky day: there were a lot of spaces open. I backed the car into a space and then read the noticeboard that explained at great length how to pay. It also listed all the possible penalties if anyone was foolish enough to do anything wrong.

[2] In many English car parks, first, we have to guess how long we expect to stay, then buy tickets to cover that amount of time, and finally display the tickets clearly in view in the window. If you come back to your car late, you can be fined. In other words, it is possible to get a parking ticket in a car park!

[3] The notice gave me the option of paying in cash at a machine that gave no change, or, more excitingly, making the transaction with my mobile phone. That sounded like fun, so I decided to give it a try. I phoned the number and started speaking to a voice, which I suspect did not belong to a real person. The voice asked me several questions, which I answered correctly, I guess. But then the voice suddenly rejected one of my answers. "What colour is your car?" it had asked. "Beige," I said, but evidently the machine was only able to accept the colour brown.

[4] "How do you spell your name?" the machine wanted to know. "O'Brien," I answered honestly, which made the voice angry. As you can see, O'Brien has two capitals and an apostrophe in it. I've had trouble with the name in Japan, but never in England, since it is a fairly common name. I finally managed to finish the call and pay my parking fee, though I felt rather unhappy about being kicked around by a piece of voice-recognition technology.

[5] After I had calmed down a bit, I looked around the car park and saw at least half a dozen people shouting into their mobiles. When I realized that the VR technology was racially and socially biased because it wouldn't accept a foreign accent, a non-programmed word, a local dialect, or the Welsh accent, and certainly anybody from Scotland, I had to smile.

Notes noticeboard「掲示板」 at great length「長々と」 parking ticket「駐車違反切符」 kick around「粗暴に扱う」 voice recognition / VR「音声認識」

A Vocabulary

Find the words in the reading that match these definitions. Write the verbs and nouns in their base forms.

1. ______________ to inform someone in advance of a possible problem (line 1)
2. ______________ to punish someone by making them pay money (line 8)
3. ______________ something available as a choice (line 10)
4. ______________ ordinary, widespread, or prevalent (line 20)
5. ______________ regional variety of a language (line 25)

B Comprehension

Rearrange the words in brackets to complete each sentence. Then write the number of the paragraph where the information is found.

1. At car parks in England, you have to pay in advance, but (careful / be / to / not / return) to your car late.
   ______________________________________ par. [ ]
2. Luckily I found a parking space in the city centre car park and then (car / began / read / the / to) park instructions.
   ______________________________________ par. [ ]
3. It was interesting to see other people also getting angry because the (accept / answers / didn't / machine / their).
   ______________________________________ par. [ ]
4. Because my name has two capitals and an apostrophe in it, the machine rejected it, (angry / feel / made / me / which).
   ______________________________________ par. [ ]
5. I wanted to pay by phone and began talking to a (didn't / everything / that / understand / voice) I said.
   ______________________________________ par. [ ]

2 Conversation

(A) As you listen to the conversation, fill in the blanks. 36

officer: I'm giving you a parking $_1$( ) because you've come back to your car ten minutes $_2$( ). And that is an offence.

driver: Oh, no! You see, there was a long $_3$( ) at the post office, and I had to post my mother's birthday present. She's $_4$( ), and she lives all by herself. If I didn't get her present to her on time, she would be very upset.

officer: Really? Well, I shouldn't do this, but I'll $_5$( ) you off.

(B) Listen and fill in the blanks in each question. Then choose the best answer. 37

1. __________ __________ the officer __________?
   (A) He is collecting a fine.
   (B) He has just finished writing a parking ticket.
   (C) He is getting into the car.
   (D) He is about to make out a parking ticket.

2. __________ __________ the __________ __________?
   (A) She doesn't have any money.
   (B) She was delayed at the post office.
   (C) She forgot the time.
   (D) The car park is a long way from the shops.

Grammar Points: 関係詞

1. 関係代名詞

I have a friend who lives in London.（ロンドンに住んでいる友人がいます）

The car that [which] is parked there is mine.（そこに停めている車は私のです）

The man whom [who] I met yesterday was an old friend of my father's.
（昨日私が会った人は、父の昔からの友人でした）

I was spoken to by a woman whose hair was gray.（白髪の女性に話しかけられました）

What he said turned out to be true.（彼の言ったことは本当であることがわかりました）

2. 関係副詞

This is the hospital where my cousin is working.（これは私のいとこが働いている病院です）

It is when she smiles that I love her best.（彼女を最も好きなのは、微笑んでいるときです）

I don't understand the reason why he is so mad.（彼がそんなに怒っている理由が理解できません）

3. 関係詞の継続用法

My daughter, who lives in Canada, emailed me this morning.
（娘はカナダに住んでいますが、今朝メールが届きました）

He told me a story, which I had already heard from Jim.
（彼は話をしてくれましたが、すでにその話をジムから聞いていました）

3 Incomplete Sentences

Choose the correct word to complete each sentence.

1. There is a car park in the centre of the city ________________ is famous for its long history.
(A) that (B) what (C) where (D) who

2. I am going to tell you the reason ________________ I got a parking ticket.
(A) what (B) when (C) where (D) why

3. I talked to a voice on the phone in the car park, ________________ did not belong to a real person.
(A) when (B) where (C) which (D) who

4. I am from England, ________________ my name is fairly common.
(A) when (B) where (C) which (D) who

5. I saw many people ________________ were shouting into their mobile phones in the car park.
(A) how (B) where (C) which (D) who

4 Text Completion

Select the best answers to complete the text.

I moved into my new flat a month ago, and I have now settled in. It is in a neighbourhood ______________ is residential. Near the station are some new flats, where I live.

1. (A) who
   (B) where
   (C) that
   (D) why

A short bus ride away there are some large houses that have beautiful gardens. There's a shopping centre ______________ you can buy almost anything you need, and there's

2. (A) that
   (B) which
   (C) who
   (D) where

a supermarket ______________ sells ready-made meals for singles like me.

3. (A) it
   (B) that
   (C) who
   (D) where

5 Keywords

Match each word or phrase with its Japanese equivalent.

1. bias	(　　)	2. change	(　　)
3. residential	(　　)	4. neighbourhood	(　　)
5. capital	(　　)	6. transaction	(　　)
7. offence	(　　)	8. ready-made meal	(　　)
9. in view	(　　)	10. settle in	(　　)

a. 違反	b. 見える所に	c. 大文字	d. 落ち着く	e. お惣菜
f. 偏見を持つ	g. 処理	h. 地区	i. おつり	j. 住宅の

Teatime

厳しい駐車制度

- イギリスは、駐車場の券売機でチケットを買うという前払い制を採用しています。おつりは出ません。そのチケットを車内の見やすいところへ置く（pay and display）システムです。屋内駐車場でも、このシステムが導入されています。しかし最近、ロンドンの中心部などでは券売機が排除され、代わりに支払い所に電話して料金を払うシステムに変更されています。
- 交通監視員（traffic warden）が巡回し、正しく駐車しているかどうかをチェックします。駐車時間を少しでも過ぎると違反切符（parking ticket）を切られ、罰金を払わなければなりません。そのため駐車時間が迫ってくると、急いで車まで走って行く人もいます。時間超過の違反罰金（parking fine）は、ロンドン市内で最高 120 ポンド、首都以外では 60 ポンドを科せられます。

Lesson 13 Weddings

comparisons, numbers

Photographs

Describe the picture by filling in the blanks in these sentences.

1. A bride is sitting on the (s   ).
2. The bride and the bridesmaids are (c   ) bouquets.

1 Reading

38

[1] Couples used to get married in their mid-twenties. But these days, they seem to be taking their time about it, so that now, 31 has become the average age to "tie the knot."

[2] Most British wedding ceremonies are held in a church, or in the town hall if it's a non-religious wedding. At both places the couple exchange vows and promise to love and honour each other "until death do them part" and so on. Japan is very similar. The couple might have a traditional ceremony in a shrine, or have a wedding that copies Western-style ceremonies, complete with a foreign priest and a choir. Another choice is the simple one: the couple fill in and sign a form at the city or ward office.

[3] Wedding receptions in Japan are quite formal. The women guests may dress up in kimono or fancy western clothes, and the men invariably look like a gathering of red-faced penguins in their formal black suits. Several people make formal speeches, which can be quite tricky because there are so many taboo phrases that must be avoided. Then there are formal toasts, more speeches, and a couple of inevitable songs. The bride in her kimono makes a quick exit and reappears in a white wedding dress. She doesn't stay around long, though, and she next appears in an eye-catching evening dress. Just as the party is getting into full swing, it finishes, and, because this is Japan, perfectly on time.

[4] The English have a much more casual approach to the reception. The bride in her wedding dress stays like that to the end. The speeches are fueled by drink and tend to be humorous and even bawdy. A party like this has a starting time, but there is no schedule for finishing it. It usually dies a natural death, sometime in the early hours of the morning.

[5] If you are thinking about getting married in England, you might want to think again. So-called "friends" like to play monstrous jokes on the young couple. The night before the wedding is often a time for the groom and his males to get drunk at a stag party. The unsuspecting groom is sometimes driven to a spot and dumped miles from home, and has to make it to the church later that day. It is great fun for everybody, except that is, for the couple.

Notes tie the knot「結婚する」 get into full swing「最高潮に達する」 fuel「勢いをつける」 die a natural death「流れ解散をする」 stag party「スタッグパーティー」結婚前に新郎の男友だちが行うパーティー make it to「～に間に合う、～にたどり着く」

A Vocabulary

Find the words in the reading that match these definitions. Write the verbs and nouns in their base forms.

1. ________________ to assure someone that you will definitely do something (line 4)
2. ________________ suitable for important occasions (line 9)
3. ________________ gorgeous; sophisticated (line 10)
4. ________________ way of doing something; method (line 17)
5. ________________ not aware of the presence of danger (line 24)

B Comprehension

Complete each sentence with a word from the box. Then write the number of the paragraph where the information is found.

clothes	finishing	increased	jokes	simplest

1. The English often play ( ) on the bride and groom. par. [ ]
2. Japanese tend to be more formal at weddings, with the bride changing her ( ) several times. par. [ ]
3. People are getting married later and later, so the marrying age has ( ) from 25 to 31. par. [ ]
4. The English are more informal, and their wedding receptions have no fixed ( ) time. par. [ ]
5. Couples may exchange vows in a ceremony in both countries, but Japan has the ( ) choice of just filling in and signing a form. par. [ ]

2 Conversation

(A) As you listen to the conversation, fill in the blanks. 39

Wendy: I hear you're going to a wedding. Who is getting 1( )?

Paul: It's the son of my 2( ), so I should go, but unfortunately the wedding is in Hawaii. I don't think many people will be able to 3( ) it there.

Wendy: How 4( )! It will be a pretty lonely wedding, won't it?

Paul: The wedding company has thought about that, so they are 5( ) local guests to the ceremony.

(B) Listen and fill in the blanks in each question. Then choose the best answer. 40

1. ________ ________ Paul ________ ________ wedding?
   (A) His boss's son is getting married. (B) His boss is getting married.
   (C) His son is getting married. (D) It is Paul's wedding.

2. ________ ________ the wedding company ________ ________ ________?
   (A) Arrange flights. (B) Attend the ceremony.
   (C) Fly to Hawaii. (D) Hire some guests.

Grammar Points: 比較、数詞

1. 比較

・比較級：語尾に -er、2 音節以上の語の前に more

My wife is one year older than I am.（妻は私より 1 歳年上です）

He is cleverer than I thought.（彼は私が思っていたよりも賢いです）

Time is more important than money to me.（私には、お金より時間のほうが大切です）

・最上級：語尾に -est、2 音節以上の語の前に most

Tokyo has the largest population in Japan.（東京は日本で最大の人口を抱えています）

That was the most difficult situation I have ever experienced.
（あれは今まで私が経験した中で最も困難な状況でした）

・原級を使った比較：「〜と同じくらい」

My little brother is as tall as I am.（弟は私と同じくらいの背の高さです）

I asked him as many questions as possible.（私は彼にできるだけ多くの質問をしました）

2. 数詞

・基数と序数

	1	2	3	4	5	12	20	21
基数	one	two	three	four	five	twelve	twenty	twenty-one
序数	first	second	third	fourth	fifth	twelfth	twentieth	twenty-first

・分数

$\frac{1}{2}$: a half, $\frac{1}{4}$: a quarter, $\frac{2}{3}$: two-thirds, $3\frac{4}{5}$: three and four-fifths

・「〜代」

He made a fortune in his twenties.（彼は 20 代でひと財産を築きました）
She was a famous actress in the nineties.（1990 年代、彼女は有名な女優でした）

3 Incomplete Sentences

Choose the correct word or phrase to complete each sentence.

1. Recently, many people are getting married in their ________________.

(A) thirties (B) thirtieth (C) thirty (D) thirty-one

2. Writing down your name at the city office is a ________________ way of getting married than having a ceremony at the shrine.

(A) simple (B) simpler (C) more simple (D) the most simple

3. Japanese wedding receptions are ________________ than English ones.

(A) as formal (B) many formal (C) more formal (D) very formal

4. He made ________________ speech I had ever heard.

(A) a humorous (B) a more humorous
(C) as humorous (D) the most humorous

5. I was ________________ as the groom at the stag party.

(A) as drunk (B) drunk (C) more drunk (D) the most drunk

4 Text Completion

Select the best answers to complete the text.

I could not imagine living in a country that was both hotter and ________________ than

1. (A) cold
   (B) colder
   (C) coldest
   (D) more cold

England. There is ________________ rain in Japan. Japan also has many earthquakes, so

2. (A) lots
   (B) many
   (C) more
   (D) several

it is ________________ more dangerous than my country. So, why do I live here and not

3. (A) much
   (B) many
   (C) lot
   (D) very

there? Well, beautiful is perhaps the answer ... by which I mean not only the country, of course, but the people, too.

5 Keywords

Match each word or phrase with its Japanese equivalent.

1.	dump	(　　)	2.	toast	(　　)
3.	bawdy	(　　)	4.	choir	(　　)
5.	invariably	(　　)	6.	monstrous	(　　)
7.	ward office	(　　)	8.	eye-catching	(　　)
9.	inevitable	(　　)	10.	so-called	(　　)

a. みだらな	b. ばかげた	c. 聖歌隊	d. 区役所	e. 乾杯
f. 人目を引く	g. いつも	h. いわゆる	i. 降ろす	j. お決まりの

Teatime

独身最後の夜

- イギリスの結婚式は、宗教に基づいて教会などで行う宗教婚（religious service）と、宗教色を排除し、役所で行う民事婚（civil service）があります。結婚式前日または数日前に、新郎（groom）と新婦（bride）はそれぞれ親しい同性の友だちを誘い、独身最後の思い出として、男性だけの Stag Night（スタッグナイト）、女性だけの Hen Night（ヘンナイト）という楽しい時間を過ごします。
- 伝統的に Stag Night や Hen Night では、近隣でパーティーをしたり、観光地へ週末の旅行に出かけたり、ローカルなパブのはしごをして、はめをはずしたり、といったことが行われています。結婚式だけでなく、Stag Night や Hen Night にもそれなりにお金がかかるのが、イギリスの結婚事情です。

Lesson 14 Dialects

subjunctives

Photographs

Describe the picture by filling in the blanks in these sentences.

1. The shop sign is upside (d   ).
2. The woman is (w   ) her dog in front of the shop.

1 Reading

41

[1] Perhaps you haven't really thought about it, but you, me, and all the people around us speak in a dialect of some sort. Maybe it's a rough, local variety, or the careful, polite speech that TV announcers use, but everyone has a dialect. Britain is only half the size of Japan in both land area and population, but you would be surprised at how many dialects there are.

[2] Your dialect can tell others where you live, what your family background is, even where you went to college. People in the south of England tend to speak with long vowels, but as you travel north, those vowels become shorter and harder. So just by listening to an English person's vowels, you can get a pretty good idea of where he or she is from.

[3] Dialects indicate status (or "class") as well as place of origin. They not only locate a person geographically, but they also "place" him or her socially. But these days, people are more mobile than they used to be. They move around a lot. They also watch a lot of TV, where they become familiar with a wide range of dialects. As a result, dialects are no longer confined to their original location or speakers—they are spreading around the country.

[4] Dialects are like fashions—they become popular for a period of time, and then, well, go out of fashion. Today's most "in vogue" dialect is called Estuary English. It is based on London's dialect, but its grammar and pronunciation are more "correct" than the original. Switch on your TV and you will see that most of the young stars and even some of the younger Royals now speak this "in" dialect.

[5] Some distinctive dialects are used to great effect both in the U.K. and in Japan. When an English comedian comes on stage and speaks in a strong, difficult-to-comprehend local dialect, such as we find in Liverpool or Yorkshire, the audience love it and are ready to laugh at anything. In Japan, the Osaka-based Yoshimoto comedy troupe uses a strong Kansai dialect with great success on national TV. People all over the country love it. Without this "strange" dialect, the comedians wouldn't get nearly so many laughs. What all this tells me is that though our languages are different, our societies really do have a lot in common.

Notes family background「家庭環境」 a wide range of「さまざまな」 in vogue「流行している」 Estuary English「河口域英語」テムズ川河口地域発祥の英語 Liverpool「リバプール」イングランド北西部マージーサイド州の都市 Yorkshire「ヨークシャー」イングランド北東部の地方 not ... nearly「到底～でない」

A Vocabulary

Find the words in the reading that match these definitions. Write the verbs in their base forms.

1.	________________	not gentle	(line 2)
2.	________________	able to move freely	(line 11)
3.	________________	to limit or restrict	(line 13)
4.	________________	free from error; true	(line 16)
5.	________________	easily recognised	(line 19)

B Comprehension

Match the beginning of each sentence (1-5) to its ending (a-e). Then write the number of the paragraph where the information is found.

1. Your dialect may indicate ________ par. [ ]
2. We all speak in a dialect, and even though Britain is small, ________ par. [ ]
3. Because of cars and TV, dialects are spreading ________ par. [ ]
4. Comedians sometimes use rough local dialects ________ par. [ ]
5. A certain dialect may become fashionable for a time, ________ par. [ ]

(a) and one that is "in" today is based on a London speaking style.
(b) away from their original locations and speakers.
(c) whether you live in the north or south of England.
(d) there are many distinctive ways of speaking.
(e) to great effect.

2 Conversation

(A) As you listen to the conversation, fill in the blanks. 42

interviewer: Thank you for coming to the $_{1}$(   ) to talk about your hometown. First of all, Simon, tell us about your early life.

Simon: My mavver says I was a $_{2}$(   ) kid, and I used to play a lot by myself ... that was in Soufend. I didn't fink too much of my teachers. But I liked $_{3}$(   ). I bough' a $_{4}$(   ) an' played it every day. And look at me now ... I'm an international $_{5}$(   ).

(B) Listen and fill in the blanks in each question. Then choose the best answer. 43

1. __________ __________ ______ person was Simon ______ ________ __________?

(A) Something of a loner. (B) He loved his school and teachers.
(C) He was a bad singer. (D) He had a lot of friends.

2. __________ __________ Simon __________?

(A) He is having an interview. (B) He is a music teacher.
(C) He is a musician. (D) He lives in London.

Notes mavver = mother Soufend = Southend fink = think bough' = bought an' = and

Grammar Points: 仮定法

1. 仮定法過去

If I had enough money, I would take a taxi.（もし十分なお金があれば、タクシーを使うのに）

If I knew his address, I could tell you.（もし彼の住所を知っていれば、教えてあげられるのに）

2. 仮定法過去完了

If I had woken up ten minutes earlier, I would have been in time.
（もし 10 分早く起きていたら、間に合っていたでしょう）

If I had not met him, I would have given up my dream.
（もし彼に会っていなかったら、夢をあきらめていたでしょう）

3. if 節と帰結節で時制が異なる場合

If he had studied harder, he would be a college student now.
（彼はもっと一生懸命勉強していたら、今頃は大学生でしょう）

If I had finished my job earlier, I would already be home now.
（もっと早く仕事を終わらせていたら、もう今頃は家にいるでしょう）

4. if 節を用いない仮定法

Without your support, I would not be here.（あなたの援助がなければ、私はここにいないでしょう）

He would have understood my idea.（彼なら私のアイデアを理解してくれたでしょう）

5. wish

I wish everyone were like you.（みんなが君のようならよいのに）

I wish you had been there.（君がそこにいたらよかったのに）

6. as if

Sometimes he acts as if he were a child.（時々彼はまるで子供であるかのように振舞います）

He looked at me as if he had never seen me.（彼は私に会ったことがないかのように見ました）

3 Incomplete Sentences

Choose the correct word or phrase to complete each sentence.

1. He talks ________________ he were a TV announcer.
   (A) as (B) as if (C) if (D) like

2. If you ________________ differently, you could conceal your educational background.
   (A) speak (B) speaking (C) spoke (D) spoken

3. ________________ cars, dialects would not have spread around the country.
   (A) As (B) For (C) To (D) Without

4. If famous people did not speak Estuary English, it ________________ “in vogue” now.
   (A) had not been (B) wasn’t (C) would not be (D) would not have been

5. If I ________________ in England longer, I could have understood English jokes better.
   (A) live (B) had lived (C) have lived (D) will live

4 Text Completion

Select the best answers to complete the text.

I'm going out for lunch now and I'll be back in an hour. If our clients ______

1. (A) asks
   (B) has
   (C) should have
   (D) will have

any questions, you have to answer them. If you can't deal with a problem, take down the details and I'll return the client's call when I get back. Don't say anything without confirmation. If I ______ you, I ______ a log of all the people you

2. (A) are
   (B) be
   (C) were
   (D) did

3. (A) would have kept
   (B) will keep
   (C) should keep
   (D) would keep

have spoken to.

5 Keywords

Match each word or phrase with its Japanese equivalent.

1. troupe ( )
2. geographically ( )
3. indicate ( )
4. for a time ( )
5. comprehend ( )
6. effect ( )
7. confirmation ( )
8. out of fashion ( )
9. based on ( )
10. deal with ( )

a. 示す　b. ～を扱う　c. すたれて　d. 確信　e. ～に基づく
f. ～を理解する　g. 効果　h. 地理的に　i. しばらくの間　j. 集団

Teatime

地域の言葉は誇り

- いまだに階級意識が強く残るイギリスでは、言葉は出身地や階級を表すと考えられています。だから、単に地域の特徴として片付けられない部分もあります。また、自分たちの言葉を誇りにして、守り続けている人たちもいます。
- ロンドンの労働者階級の人が話す Cockney（コクニー）では、[θ] は [f]、[ð] は [v] になります。例えば、three は [fríː]、with は [wiv] と発音します。バーミンガムの言葉は Brummie（ブルミー）、リバプールの言葉は Scouse（スカウス）と呼ばれ、地域独特の発音があります。
- 分かりにくいのが北東部の方言で、特にニューカッスルの言葉は Geordie（ジョーディー）と呼ばれ、イギリス人でも理解できないことがあります。例えば "Divvent dee tha!"（Don't do that!）と言われると、何を言っているのか分かりません。

Lesson 15 Winter Warmth

voices (active voice, passive voice)

Photographs

Describe the picture by filling in the blanks in these sentences.

1. A woman and her child are sitting on the snow in front of a (s   ).
2. The mother is (m   ) a snowball.

1 Reading

44

[1] Isn't Japan an interesting place? When first I arrived in this country, I couldn't believe how hot the summers could be—34°C—and how cold and snowy the winters. Northern Japan can get huge snowfalls, sometimes even burying large houses, but life goes on. Yet when a blizzard hits the cities along the Pacific coast, life grinds to a halt. Trains stop, planes are grounded, classes are cancelled, people struggle to get to work.

[2] In Britain, when and where heavy snow will come is unpredictable, so nobody prepares for the worst. Traffic stops and railways become immobile. The official excuse always seems to be, "It is the wrong kind of snow."

[3] Like its other seasons, Japan's winter arrives almost overnight. The air is suddenly different—very cold and windy, with a hint of snow falling not far away. England's seasons change more slowly: it takes some time for winter to set in, but once it has arrived, you feel cold to the bone. People look down at their feet while they walk and forget to smile. How do Britain and Japan cope with this unpleasant season?

[4] The traditional English house is made of brick, so when you use the heater for a long time, the house stays warm. Most houses have a central heating system. A single gas, electric or oil heater pushes hot water through pipes around the whole house, so that every room becomes warm. Japan has a different approach. Here, most houses are built to combat the summer heat, which means that the walls lose heat in winter. Usually, only the rooms being used at the time are heated. The other rooms are freezing! But most likely, you have a kotatsu or two in your house. That little heater under the table is simple, cheap, and beautifully functional. I can't understand why it hasn't become the world's best-selling product.

[5] Food in Japan changes with the seasons, too. Often, the evening meal is a hotpot, or nabe, that sits in the middle of the dining table bubbling and boiling away, making the room warm and steamy. And eating this "boiled dinner," we feel "toasty" and comfortable. But best of all, on a cold winter's night, soaking in a deep, hot Japanese bath warms us as we get ready to go to bed and call it a day.

Notes grind to a halt「急停止する、麻痺する」 ground「地上に止める、飛ばない」 to the bone「骨まで」 boiled dinner「鍋料理」 call it a day「１日を終える」

A Vocabulary

Find the words in the reading that match these definitions. Write the verbs and nouns in their base forms.

1. ________________ to cover or hide something completely (line 3)
2. ________________ to get ready (line 6)
3. ________________ a small indication or suggestion (line 10)
4. ________________ to take action to reduce or prevent (line 17)
5. ________________ an article that is manufactured for sale (line 21)

B Comprehension

Rearrange the words in brackets to complete each sentence. Then write the number of the paragraph where the information is found.

1. In Britain, central heating makes the whole house warm, but the Japanese (heat / one / only / tend / to) or two rooms.
   ____ par. [ ]
2. Because in Britain, it is hard to predict when snow will fall, (for / is / it / nobody / prepared), so transport stops.
   ____ par. [ ]
3. In northern Japan, life goes on even in the midst of a blizzard, but along the Pacific coast, even (a / can / disrupt / little / snow) our daily activities.
   ____ par. [ ]
4. In Japan, the old-style way of life in winter is to (a / eat / food / in / served) hotpot and to take a deep hot bath, then go to bed.
   ____ par. [ ]
5. Britain's seasons change more slowly than those in Japan, and winter (cold / feel / horribly / makes / you).
   ____ par. [ ]

2 Conversation

(A) As you listen to the conversation, fill in the blanks. 45

forecaster: Good morning, and here is the weather forecast for Friday 13th. It was a very cold night with a thick 1( ). Later today, the north of England will probably have snow 2( ), with the snow becoming quite 3( ) in the evening.

man: Oh dear. I was going to drive up the motorway to Manchester today, but I guess I'll have to 4( ) the train. Now then, I'd better check the computer for the train 5( ), and then phone my office.

(B) Listen and fill in the blanks in each question. Then choose the best answer. 46

1. ________ ________ they have a ________ ________ ________?
   (A) On Friday. (B) Today. (C) In the south. (D) In the north.

2. ________ ________ he ________ ________ Manchester?
   (A) By air. (B) By car. (C) By train. (D) On foot.

Grammar Points: 態（能動態、受動態）

1. 能動態と受動態

He wrote this letter.（彼がこの手紙を書きました）
This letter was written by him.（この手紙は彼によって書かれました）

Mary sent Jim an invitation card.（メアリーはジムに招待状を送りました）
Jim was sent an invitation card by Mary.（ジムはメアリーから招待状を送られました）

Mary sent an invitation card to Jim.（メアリーはジムに招待状を送りました）
An invitation card was sent to Jim by Mary.（招待状がメアリーからジムに送られました）

Everybody calls him Chuck.（みんなは彼のことをチャックと呼びます）
He is called Chuck by everybody.（彼はみんなにチャックと呼ばれています）

2. 進行形の受動態

The lift is being checked.（エレベーターは点検中です）

His house is being remodeled now.（彼の家は今リフォーム中です）

3. get を用いた受動態

I got totally drunk last night.（昨夜、完全に酔っぱらっていました）

Nobody got hurt in the accident.（その事故でけが人はいませんでした）

3 Incomplete Sentences

Choose the correct word or phrase to complete each sentence.

1. Sometimes in northern Japan, large houses ________________ in heavy snow.
   (A) are buried (B) burying (C) gets buried (D) is buried

2. Heavy snow had not ________________, so no one was ready for it.
   (A) be predicted (B) been predicted (C) was predicted (D) predicted

3. A few inches of snow will ________________ by midnight.
   (A) are seen (B) be seen (C) been seen (D) see

4. A new heating system ________________ in my house now.
   (A) be installed (B) installed (C) installing (D) is being installed

5. We had a hotpot dinner and got nicely ________________.
   (A) warm up (B) warming up (C) warmed up (D) was warmed up

4 Text Completion

Select the best answers to complete the text.

My oldest son Dave came home from university last night. We hadn't seen him for over half a year, and you'd never guess what he looked like. He had let his hair grow long and it ______________ dyed in red and white stripes. I ______________ at his face, too.

1. (A) had been
   (B) had being
   (C) is having
   (D) was having

2. (A) surprise
   (B) surprised
   (C) was surprised
   (D) was surprising

His eyebrows ______________ to two thin lines and he had a nose ring and a scruffy beard!

3. (A) trimmed
   (B) were trimmed
   (C) were trimming
   (D) had trimmed

I wonder if he will ever grow up!

5 Keywords

Match each word with its Japanese equivalent.

1.	motorway	(　　)	2.	eyebrow	(　　)
3.	toasty	(　　)	4.	unpredictable	(　　)
5.	trim	(　　)	6.	steamy	(　　)
7.	dye	(　　)	8.	functional	(　　)
9.	hotpot	(　　)	10.	immobile	(　　)

a. 染める　b. 鍋料理　c. 予測できない　d. 動かない　e. 剃り込む
f. 温かく心地よい　g. 高速道路　h. 機能的な　i. まゆげ　j. 湯気が立ちこめた

Teatime

冬の暖房

- イギリスでは、ほとんどの家はセントラル・ヒーティングで暖房をします。これはボイラーで水を沸かし、その熱湯を配管で循環させます。温水が各部屋の convector（対流暖房器）と呼ばれるパネルを流れると、そのパネルが熱くなり部屋の空気が暖かくなるのです。
- 最近の新築の flat（アパート）では、Economy 7（エコノミー 7）という電気による暖房様式も多く見られます。電気代の安い夜から深夜にかけて空気を暖め、その暖かい空気で暖房します。
- イギリスのガス・電気代は基本料金がよく値上がりするので、暖房費は非常に高くつきます。寝るときは湯たんぽで身体を温めたり、家の中でコートを着て生活するイギリス人もいます。

Viewpoints: Japan and England すっきり日英比較		[B-770]
1　刷	2015年 1月 15日	
4　刷	2024年 4月 25日	
著　者	テリー・オブライエン	Terry O'Brien
	三原　京	Kei Mihara
	立本　秀洋	Shuyo Tatemoto
	木村　博是	Hiroshi Kimura
発行者	南雲　一範　Kazunori Nagumo	
発行所	株式会社　南雲堂 〒162-0801　東京都新宿区山吹町361 NAN'UN-DO Co., Ltd. 361 Yamabuki-cho, Shinjuku-ku, Tokyo 162-0801, Japan 振替口座 : 00160-0-46863 TEL: 03-3268-2311(代表)／FAX: 03-3269-2486	
編　集	加藤　敦	
製　版	木内　早苗	
装　丁	Nスタジオ	
検　印	省　略	
コード	ISBN 978-4-523-17770-8　C0082	

Printed in Japan

E-mail　nanundo@post.email.ne.jp
URL　https://www.nanun-do.co.jp/

音声で学ぶリーディングで得点力アップ！

TOEFL® Test iBT リーディング 実践編

TOEFL® Test iBT Reading: Practice for Success

Jim Knudsen ／ 生井　健一

A5判　320ページ　定価（本体2200円＋税）　CD2枚付

TOEFL iBTのリーディング・セクションの効果的練習教材！
合わせてリスニングにも使えるCD音声を用意した。

特徴

- 比較・対照、因果関係など、北米大学での勉強の際に必ず読むことになる文章のパターンを研究し、様々な読解難易度のオリジナル・パッセージを多様な分野から用意した。
- 練習問題はマルチティプル・チョイスはもちろん、iBTより始まった新しい形式の設問（情報を類別する、サマリーを完成する等）も備えている。
- iBTでは難しい単語はクリックして、その定義を参照できるようになっているが、本書でもGlossaryを用意して、必要に応じて活用できるようにした。